STRATEGIES
FOR TEACHING
PHYSICAL EDUCATION

LINUS J. DOWELL
Texas A & M University

PRENTICE-HALL, INC., Englewood Cliffs, New Jersey

Library of Congress Cataloging in Publication Data

DOWELL, LINUS J   1930-
  Strategies for teaching physical education.

  Bibliography: p.
  1. Physical education and training—Study and
teaching.   I. Title.
GV361.D68   613.7′07′1273   74-9724
ISBN 0-13-850974-3

Printed in the United States of America.

10 9 8 7 6 5 4 3 2 1

PRENTICE-HALL INTERNATIONAL, INC., London
PRENTICE-HALL OF AUSTRALIA, PTY. LTD., Sydney
PRENTICE-HALL OF CANADA, LTD., Toronto
PRENTICE-HALL OF INDIA PRIVATE LIMITED, New Delhi
PRENTICE-HALL OF JAPAN, INC., Tokyo

CONTENTS

PREFACE

Since becoming a member of the physical education profession some twenty years ago, I have served in the United States Navy; as a coach; as a teacher of health, physical education, and recreation courses at the undergraduate and graduate level; as department head of Health, Physical Education, and Recreation, and presently as professor of Health and Physical Education at Texas A&M University. During this time I have observed that there is something less than competency in the area of physical education teaching, techniques, and methods.

There has been considerable controversy over the value of courses in "Methods of Teaching." Some claim that teachers are born, not made. Others say that anyone who knows the subject matter can teach it. It would be foolish to claim that personality factors do not affect teaching or that a teacher can teach something of which he is ignorant. Strategies for teaching are not a crutch for poor skills and/or scholarship, but neither is skill and/or scholarship a substitute for teaching competency. This text takes the view that any skilled, intelligent well-adjusted, mature person can learn to teach, and every experienced teacher can always improve in teaching.

This text was written for teachers, describing strategies for teaching physical education to secondary school students. Emphasis is given to procedures for good teaching in physical education. It is hoped that this text and the Performance Manual will contribute to the teaching competency of physical education teachers.

I wish to acknowledge gratitude to the many associates, students as well as faculty, at Northeast Missouri State University, the United States Naval Academy Preparatory School, the University of Missouri, Arkansas State University, and Texas A&M University, who over the years have furnished stimulation, suggestion, and criticism in the development of my professional thinking. Special appreciation is given to Dr. Ralph K. Watkins, University of Missouri, for his early inspiration and sensitiveness to strategies for teaching.

Linus J. Dowell

1

PLANNING FOR TEACHING

Teaching physical education is skilled work. It is not true that we are naturally endowed with the ability to teach—without learning how or without practicing. People who are untrained should no more expect to be able to teach effectively than people who have never learned and never practiced can expect to find themselves good football players, basketball players, golfers, etc.

Those who are in earnest in wishing to learn to teach physical education effectively should face their task in the spirit in which they would set themselves to learn the rules, to learn the techniques, and to practice some new game.

The purpose of this chapter is to set the stage for teaching. As an old football coach once said, "Over half of my time must be spent in organization if I am to be an effective coach."

THE ACADEMIC SETTING

Secondary school teaching is a noble profession. *Secondary education* consists of that education provided for pupils customarily enrolled in school grades seven through fourteen. Secondary schools are commonly organized into administrative units housed in one building, or a group of buildings and administratively responsible to one administrative official, usually the high school principal.

The secondary school administrative units commonly found in the United States are:

1. The *four-year high school,* including grades nine through twelve.
2. The *junior high school,* including grades seven through nine.
3. The *senior high school,* including grades ten through twelve.
4. The *six-year high school* (sometimes called the Junior-Senior High School), including grades seven through twelve.
5. The *junior college,* commonly including grades thirteen and fourteen.
6. The *four-year junior college,* including grades eleven through fourteen.

The *school program* consists of all those experiences provided and administered by the school that purport to have educational value. The school program includes: courses (Physical Education I, English II, Algebra I, etc.); athletics (football, basketball, track, etc.); clubs (math club, science club, etc.); extra-curricular activities (band, junior-senior prom, all-school play, etc.).

A *curriculum* consists of those experiences planned to meet the needs of a school group having some degree of homogeneity. A college curriculum would be a high school curriculum designed for entry into college. A vocational curriculum might be designed to enable one to be an automobile mechanic. A curriculum might also be defined as a set of experiences or offerings needed for graduation.

Subject areas are classification of large groupings of related subjects, such as English, Mathematics, Physical Education, etc.

A *secondary school course* consists of a school year's experiences in some recognized subject. Courses are generally scheduled to meet one period per day, five days a week, for one school year.

Half-courses may meet one period per day, five days a week, for one semester or one period per day, two or three days per week, for a school year.

A *unit* consists of the planning of the experiences of pupils around a theme or center of organization that has significance and wholeness for the pupils, such as a unit in basketball, a unit in dance, a unit in physical fitness, etc. A unit may be *concentrated* (e.g., a unit in touch football that continues daily for six weeks) or a unit may be *distributed* (e.g., a unit in physical fitness that may have certain days set aside such as Tuesdays and Thursdays or a portion of each period), each continuing throughout the school year.

GOALS

An effective teacher must have goals for herself/himself and the class. Goals may be derived in many ways; pupil-teacher participation, pupil-determined, teacher-determined, etc., but a class and teacher must have goals if teaching is to be effective.

It is impossible to plan a trip unless you know where you are going. Likewise you cannot expect specific outcomes in a class unless you have planned for them. Each physical education teacher must have clearly in mind the characteristics of a physically educated person before he can plan to move a class in that direction (C/P 1); see Competency/Performance 1 in *Performance Manual* for *Strategies for Teaching Physical Education*).

When is a person physically educated? The obvious answer of course is that a person is never really physically educated, but this shouldn't hinder us in our attempt to reach this goal. A 10-flat hundred runner may never become a 9.5 sprinter but it helps him to improve if he has a lofty goal. Needless to say, each physical educator must define a physically educated person in his or her own way. Some of the common attributes of a physically educated person as expressed by many physical educators indicate that a *physically educated* person must:

1. Have a zest for living.
2. Be able to save himself from drowning.
3. Be able to perform two or more team sports with above average ability.
4. Be able to perform two or more individual sports with above average ability.
5. Exercise regularly.
6. Maintain a high level of physical fitness.
7. Be able to move to rhythm.
8. Be able to move gracefully through space.
9. Be able to change directions and vary speed with agility.
10. Know the benefits of exercise.
11. Know how to care for the body at any age.

COURSE LAYOUTS

A *course layout* is a concise planning of a high school course in terms of the units that constitute the course. It consists of a listing of the units by unit title, the arrangement of units in sequence, an estimation of the time needed for each unit, and the course title. In physical education, activities such as football, basketball, etc., make up the units of a course.

Planning course layouts is an important part in organization for teaching. One should report to the school well before school begins in order to have time to do the necessary paper work. When reporting for a new position you should familiarize yourself with the community before finding a place to live; get to know the grocer, banker, filling station operator, etc., in town; locate the recreation areas (parks, playgrounds, recreation centers, bowling alleys, rod and gun clubs, pool halls, skating rinks, archery clubs, etc.); try to find out what activities students participate in during their spare time and what adults in the community do for recreation (C/P 2).

Before constructing course layouts, appropriate activities for the classes to be taught should be listed (C/P 3). This implies that all activities are listed for which equipment and facilities are available at the school and in the community. Once a list of the activities that may be included in the physical education program is completed and the school program offerings of previous years have been identified, activities which meet stated objectives need to be determined (C/P 4). Identification of the activities which best meet objectives may be evaluated through the use of an activity evaluation format (C/P 5 and C/P 6).

Before laying out the final draft of a physical education program there are several principles that need to be considered. A sound physical education program must:

1. Be based on the age, sex, needs, capabilities, and interests of students.
2. Make the best use of available resources (teachers' abilities, facilities, and equipment) in the school and community.
3. Include lifetime sports as well as meet present activity needs.
4. Be flexible and provide for student elective choice of activities.
5. Be coeducational in part.
6. Provide for various types of activities: dance, recreational, aquatics, self-testing, team, dual, and individual.
7. Provide for all levels of skill: beginning, intermediate, and advanced.
8. Provide for evaluation of progress toward stated goals.
9. Include more team activities in the beginning years of secondary school and more individual and dual activities in the advanced years of secondary school.
10. Provide activities in the proper learning sequence.
11. Provide a minimum of fifteen different activities in order to meet the required criteria in the secondary school.

After appropriate activities have been selected, the above principles must be integrated with certain administrative considerations. For example, each physical education course, e.g., Physical Education I (Freshman), Physical Education II (Sophomore), Physical Education III (Junior), and Physical Education IV (Senior), should contain students at the same grade level, or students should be grouped according to their ability. In many schools, however, administrators are reluctant to classify students in physical education according to grade or ability. Administrative decisions affect the physical education program and therefore partially determine the matrix for constructing course layouts.

The following are examples of course layouts for a four-year high school in which freshmen, sophomores, juniors, and seniors are administratively assigned to the same class (i.e., cannot be separated by grade).

EXAMPLE: CONSECUTIVE YEAR PLANS

PHYSICAL EDUCATION I	
19—0	
Touch football	9 weeks
Basketball	9 weeks
Recreational games	9 weeks
Tennis	9 weeks

PHYSICAL EDUCATION II	
19—1	
Speedball	9 weeks
Tumbling	9 weeks
Swimming	9 weeks
Softball	9 weeks

PHYSICAL EDUCATION III	
19—2	
Soccer	9 weeks
Rebound tumbling	9 weeks
Dance	9 weeks
Track and field	9 weeks

PHYSICAL EDUCATION IV	
19—3	
Physical fitness	9 weeks
Gymnastics	9 weeks
Volleyball	9 weeks
Golf	9 weeks

If the administration could be persuaded to group freshmen with sophomores and juniors with seniors in the same classes, a progression of activities might be worked out as indicated below:

EXAMPLE: ALTERNATE YEAR PLANS

19–0			
FRESHMAN-SOPHOMORE		**JUNIOR-SENIOR**	
Touch football I	6 weeks	Soccer	6 weeks
Swimming I	6 weeks	Basketball II	6 weeks
Square dance	6 weeks	Recreational games	6 weeks
Tumbling I	6 weeks	Gymnastics	6 weeks
Track and field I	6 weeks	Badminton	6 weeks
Softball	6 weeks	Tennis II	6 weeks

19–1			
FRESHMAN-SOPHOMORE		**JUNIOR-SENIOR**	
Speedball	6 weeks	Touch football II	6 weeks
Basketball I	6 weeks	Tumbling II	6 weeks
Rebound tumbling	6 weeks	Social Dance	6 weeks
Volleyball	6 weeks	Swimming II	6 weeks
Physical fitness	6 weeks	Track and field II	6 weeks
Tennis I	6 weeks	Golf	6 weeks

Course layouts when students are administratively assigned to classes according to grade level might appear as follows:

EXAMPLE: YEARLY PLANS

PHYSICAL EDUCATION I		PHYSICAL EDUCATION II	
Touch football I	6 weeks	Touch football II	6 weeks
Soccer I	6 weeks	Speedball	6 weeks
Basketball I	6 weeks	Dance I	6 weeks
Physical fitness	distributive	Rebound tumbling	6 weeks
Tumbling	6 weeks	Physical fitness	distributive
Swimming I	6 weeks	Volleyball	6 weeks
Track and field	6 weeks	Softball	6 weeks

PHYSICAL EDUCATION III		PHYSICAL EDUCATION IV	
Soccer II	6 weeks	Touch football III	6 weeks
Swimming II	6 weeks	Recreational games	6 weeks
Basketball II	6 weeks	Basketball III	6 weeks
Badminton	6 weeks	Dance II	6 weeks
Physical fitness	distributive	Physical fitness IV	distributive
Tennis I	6 weeks	Golf II	6 weeks
Golf	6 weeks	Tennis II	6 weeks

Modifications of course layouts must take into account administrative procedures, activity season, needs and interests of students, learning sequence, equipment and facilities available, teacher qualifications, community mores, and other principles of program planning. As can readily be seen, it is impossible to set up an "ideal" program, for each program must be unique to a particular school (C/P 7).

TEACHING PLANS

A *source unit* (C/P 8) is a plan that is developed for the teacher's use. The source unit commonly sets the limits, suggests the organization, and outlines in detail the subject matter to be used. Generally a source unit in physical education includes history, nomenclature, terms, playing area, players, nature of the activity, rules and regulations, safety precautions, skills, teaching points, individual drills, group drills, combination drills and lead-up games. Any knowledges concerning the activity to be taught should appear in the source unit. An outline of a source unit in basketball might include the following:

Title: **Basketball**

History of the game
Description of the game
   Nature of the game
   Playing court
   Equipment
   Players
   Time
   Scoring
   Putting the ball in play
   Dribbling

Traveling
Out of bounds
Violations
Fouls
Penalty
Fundamental techniques and skills
Catching
Passing
Overhand pass
Two-hand chest pass
Bounce pass
Hook pass
Two-hand underhand pass
Two-hand overhead pass
Dribbling
Feinting
Pivoting
Screening
Shooting
One-hand push shot
Two-hand set shot
Hook shot
Lay-up shot
Pivot shot
Foul shot
Defensive play
Stance for defense
Types of defense
Zone defense
Man-to-man defense
Press
Offensive play
Types of offense
Man-to-man
Zone
Press
Individual strategy

A *unit layout* (C/P 9) is a brief overall plan for the unit. It consists of the concise planning of a unit in terms of the skills and cognitive material to be taught each day of the unit. The sequence of activity, skills, drills, teaching aids, and techniques to be used are included in the unit layout as they appear for each class period. A day's entry for a unit in tumbling might include:

```
Drill:   Forward roll
         Backward roll
         Kip-up
Teach:   Two-man forward roll
         Two-man backward roll
         Hand-head stand
```

A *handout* (C/P 10) is prepared by the teacher when the school does not adopt a textbook for physical education. Normally the handout consists of the nomenclature, terms, nature of the activity, basic rules and regulations, and any other items that students need to know in order to meet the objectives of the unit.

A handout in tennis might include:

Title: Tennis

The court
Equipment
Players and preliminaries
Serving
Order of serving
Returning a ball
Out of bounds
Scoring
The game
The set
The match
When players change sides
Points to remember in singles play
Points to remember in doubles play
Tennis strategy
Tennis terminology
Bibliography

EVALUATION

Written Achievement Tests [1]

Written achievement tests evaluate knowledge in physical education. Knowledge may be evaluated in several ways, however, and with large classes objective tests have been the most widely used due to the time saved in grading.

---

[1] See Margaret J. Safrit, *Evaluation in Physical Education* (Englewood Cliffs, N.J.: Prentice-Hall, Inc., 1973), pp. 175–202, for further guidelines.

The types of objective items which are best suited for testing physical education activities include multiple-choice items, matching items, and true-false items. Before making up a written test, the teacher must first determine what knowledge is to be developed in the unit; what kinds of knowledge should be tested to determine the ability of the students to do the activity for which the teaching has been given; and having identified the subject matter to be tested, what types of test items will best evaluate knowledge of the subject matter?

Objective items (multiple-choice, matching, true-false) do not attempt to test the student's ability to organize and present his knowledge in his own language, but test the student's recognition of the correct answer among possible choices. These tests do not indicate for certain whether the student would have recalled the correct answer without any hints.

In any written achievement test avoid asking questions which can be answered solely on the basis of intelligence without need for specific knowledge of the subject tested and in like manner avoid asking questions about trivial details and useless subjects.

Multiple-choice items (C/P 11-2) consist of a statement followed by a series of choices. Multiple-choice items may be used effectively in physical education activities to present strategy situations involving reasoning based on knowledge. Such items require the student to use his knowledge rather than to demonstrate his memory for small, detailed facts. An example of a multiple-choice item in football might be:

_____ 1. While waiting in a position for the snap, the offensive lineman should:
    A. look at the ball
    B. look at the man he is to block
    C. look at an object down field
    D. close his eyes and listen

Ingenuity in the construction of items adds to their interest and usefulness. Diagrams, plays, positions, or pictures add reality to test items and bring them closer to practical situations. For example:

_____ 1. The gymnastic performer in the drawing at the right is in a:
    A. layout position
    B. tuck position
    C. pike position
    D. seat drop position

Criteria for constructing good multiple-choice items include:

1. Answers to be written on the same page with the test item should appear

to the left of the number of the initial statement and be identified by a capital letter.

2. There should be only one correct and undisputed answer.

3. Each item should test only one idea.

4. All choices should represent possible answers and deal with similar ideas.

5. Ordinarily, no fewer than four nor more than six choices should be used.

6. As much of the item as possible should appear in the introductory statement.

7. Choices following the introductory statement should complete the statement in good grammatical fashion.

8. Care should be taken when using "a" or "an" as the final word in the introductory statement where it might give a clue to the answer.

9. Possible choices should be listed in a column.

10. Plausible choices should be used so that any one might be picked if the answer is not known.

11. In choices where numbers appear, arrange in order of magnitude.

Matching items (C/P 11–3) are elongated multiple-choice items, and most rules that apply to constructing good multiple-choice items also apply to construction of matching items. Matching items are best used in testing definitions of terms, nomenclature, and recognition of positions in physical education. A matching item consists of five to twelve numbered statements in the left-hand column to be matched with from eight to seventeen words or phrases in the right-hand column preceded by capital letters. A matching item in tennis might look like the following:

_____ 1. Striking the ball with the racket	A. Ace
_____ 2. Score of 40-all	B. Let
	C. Volley
_____ 3. Six games, provided one player wins by two or more	D. Deuce
	E. Fault
_____ 4. Same as no score	F. Love
_____ 5. Server won one point after 40-all	G. Smash
	H. Drop shot
_____ 6. Replay of ball on any questionable decision on any point of play	I. Serve
	J. Lob
_____ 7. Loss of point due to an error	K. Stroke
_____ 8. Ball hit before it touches the court	L. Set
	M. Save
_____ 9. Ball hit high and over the opponent's head	N. Add-out
_____ 10. A hard hit return of a lob	O. Add-in

Basic rules for constructing good matching items include:

1. Construct the matching items around one subject; don't mix names, dates, and places.
2. Don't give clues to the answer by mixing plural and singular nouns.
3. Mix up order of statements and answers.
4. Have at least five but no more than twelve statements for each matching item.
5. The column containing the answers should have three to five more possible choices than statements to be matched.
6. If any answer may be used more than once the directions to the matching item should state "any answer may be used more than once."
7. All parts of the matching item should appear on the same page.
8. Answers should be placed in a column to the left of the number of the statement to be answered.
9. Capital rather than lower case letters should be used to identify answers.

True-false items (C/P 11–1) are the most commonly used items but good true-false statements are not easy to construct. Statements taken from textbooks do not usually make good true-false items. Examples of true-false items in speed-ball follow:

T F 1. The ball is put into play by a jump ball in the middle of the playing field to start the game.

T F 2. Defensive players on the kickoff must remain behind the restraining line until the ball is kicked.

Criteria for construction of true-false items follow:

1. Don't have part of the item contain a true idea and another part a false idea. Make the statement all true or all false.
2. Avoid double negatives.
3. Avoid using words such as "all," "only," "always," "generally," "usually," etc., in the statement unless these words are an important part of the student's understanding, as they might give a hint to the answer.
4. Make about half of the items true and about half of the items false.
5. Have the answers thoroughly mixed. Don't have them in any set pattern.
6. Don't make true statements consistently longer than false statements or vice versa.
7. Construct a method of answering true-false questions that is objective.

Either have students circle T or F or place + or 0 in the blank to indicate true or false.

Criteria for construction of a written achievement test follow:

1. In a single test, use no more than two or three different types of items.
2. Prepare more items than will be used in the final test.
3. Include some reasonably easy items and some fairly difficult items.
4. Whenever possible arrange items in order of difficulty, starting with the easier items. Generally those items easiest to answer are listed first and then the rest in order of difficulty, such as true-false, multiple-choice, and matching.
5. Organize test items for rapid scoring, usually in a column.
6. Provide clear, precise directions for answering each type item.
7. Choose the type of test item that best evaluates that particular bit of subject matter. Try not to duplicate specific points.
8. State in the directions the value given each correct answer.
9. Scatter the position of correct answers.

Skill Tests

Skill tests (C/P 12) are commonly used in physical education to help evaluate performance. Teacher-made tests are probably as good as most of the standardized tests in existence, since the validity and reliability of skill tests are not high. There are two major considerations in evaluating skill by testing: construction and administration. Steps in the construction of a skill test include:

1. Determining the essential skills that students must be able to perform in order to do the activity in which they are being instructed.
2. Selecting the tasks that best represent the significant aspects of the performance to be tested.
3. Deciding upon what basis good and poor performance will be determined (quality of the finished activity, skill and accuracy of movement, speed, combinations, etc.).

A skill test should include:

Title
Equipment
Scorers
Recorders

Stations
Description of tasks
Forms for collecting scores
Method of objectively scoring test

Criteria for administering a skill test would include:

1. Determining the most effective, consistent, and economical way to give the test.
2. Determining how long it will take a class to complete all items of the test.
3. Determining the equipment needed.
4. Deciding where to station all equipment in order to insure a smooth, steady flow of students from one task to another.
5. Determining the assistance needed for giving the test.
6. Instructing students and assistants as to their duties as timekeepers, scorers, etc.
7. Securing score sheets, record forms, or check lists to give a uniform scoring procedure.
8. Testing all groups in exactly the same way and scoring every student on the same basis.

Peer Evaluation

As subjective as it may seem, peer evaluation is probably one of the most useful methods of evaluating ability in team sports for physical education classes. If teams have played a round-robin tournament where every team has at one time or another played every other team during the physical education class period, a peer evaluation of skill is most helpful. Peer evaluation consists of the teacher asking each student to list in order of playing ability the four students on his team who he feels are the better players. For obvious reasons the teacher would instruct each student not to include himself in the evaluation. Each student will also list eight opposing players in order of playing ability. By reversing the values of each vote and summing up the scores for each student, those with the highest scores should be the better performers and those with the lower scores will be among the weaker players. As subjective as this method may appear it is a valuable instrument in evaluation of skill in physical education activities.

DAILY PLANS

Daily plans assist teachers in keeping material in proper order, help to avoid omitting essential information, act as a timetable for instruction, and help to keep proper emphasis on the various items to be covered.

The *daily time schedule* is the precise planning of specific activities for a class during a particular period.

A Daily Time Schedule (C/P 13) is the teacher's plan for a particular class in the gymnasium or on the playing field. It should include:

Period
Grade
Objectives
Equipment and materials needed
A layout of the area and location of equipment
A time schedule of instruction
Skills and teaching points
Drill diagrams and practice routines

Daily Lesson Plans (C/P 14) are constructed by the teacher as an aid in classroom teaching. Daily lesson plans for class instruction include:

Title
Objectives
Learning aids
References
Introduction
  Motivation
  Scope of lesson
  Value of lesson
  Method used
  Student comprehension
Outline of subject matter
  Notes on method and techniques
  Suggestions on teacher activity (use of aids, etc.)
  Suggestions for student activity (students work problem . . .)
  Questions to be asked
Application
  Application of skills, knowledge taught, etc.
  Drills
Summary
  Recapitulation
  Reorganization of material for students
  Strengthening of weak spots in instruction

Identification of test items
Assignment

A good teacher knows where he is going and how to get there. Planning for teaching is tedious, hard work, but will result in tremendous dividends long before the semester is over in terms of teaching effectiveness.

2

TECHNIQUES AND METHODS
OF TEACHING

There is a story about a man who went to get some water and took a sieve in which to carry it. As you can imagine, his success was negligible. Somebody had to come along and change the method of carrying water by lining the sieve with clay before the objective could be reached. Insight into the problem indicated affixing a handle to the sieve so that water could be transported faster and thus the objective reached in a shorter period of time. As fantastic as it may seem, a great many teachers "carry water in a sieve."

In the illustration above, the water is the subject matter, the carrier is the teacher, the way it is carried (container) is the method, and the handle and clay used to make the method of carrying water more effective are the techniques.

Techniques of teaching are devices employed by the teacher to better carry the subject matter. In the discussion method of teaching, the teacher might employ the question-and-answer technique or the oral-report technique. If a teacher used the lecture-demonstration method of teaching, the teacher demonstration technique might be used, the student demonstration technique might be used, or the loop film demonstration technique might be used. The teaching technique, then, is the specific way a teaching method is put into practice. Methods and techniques of teaching are selected in terms of the subject matter to be taught and modified to fit the individual learner or group of learners.

GENERAL TECHNIQUES

There are so many teaching techniques available to teachers of physical education today that whole textbooks might be written in this area. Professional journals are full of techniques for effective teaching that can be applied to most any situation if teachers will put forth some effort to utilize them in their programs. No longer is the physical education teacher limited to mere sports equipment: he/she now has available numerous ways to present skills instruction, game strategies, and general information in order to fulfill the objectives of physical education.

Knowledge of the fundamentals and rules must initially be *presented* by the instructor. After the presentation of rules and basic fundamentals, the students must have a chance to apply these through *participation*. If the instructor is a skilled performer, he will be able to demonstrate to the class. The instructor should use practice time to give *individual instruction* and correction. *Interaction* with each student should point out how much success the instructor had in teaching skills. By *observing* the students, the instructor should be able to note each student's weak and strong points.

A more concrete understanding of why a skill is performed a certain way may aid in learning through the *mechanical analysis* of the skill. Students may be *assigned* certain tasks outside of class or asked to give *oral reports* to the class in an attempt to improve learning. Teachers may employ the *questioning* technique to give feedback as to learning progress. Generally the teacher asks the question to the class as a whole, waits until all have had time to formulate an answer, and then calls on only one student to respond. This technique allows all the students to think of how they would answer the question.

AUDIO-VISUAL TECHNIQUES

The use of teaching aids and materials is a technique of teaching which supplements the learning process. Students who are not stimulated by other teaching techniques may be motivated by films, charts, or other resource materials. Highly skilled students may broaden the scope of their knowledge by studying more complex audio-visual materials. Audio-visual aids are not a substitute for a well-qualified physical education teacher but if carefully selected, properly prepared, smoothly integrated into the lesson, and constantly evaluated, they will contribute to the learning process.

Picture, Graph, and Diagram Techniques

There are many different ways of producing and using instructional visuals in the locker room or gymnasium. Among these are still pictures, pictorial displays, charts, graphs, diagrams, murals, and cartoons. Visuals are valuable for a number of reasons: (1) they easily attract attention and tend to arouse interest; (2) they can be used to illustrate relationships, similarities, and contrasts between aspects of physical education activities; and (3) they can convey messages that are very hard to put into words.

Probably the most readily available and widely used visual in physical education is the still picture. Still pictures tend to stimulate interest and raise questions about the activity. One important advantage that still pictures have over films and television is that students can have a relatively long period of time to analyze the pictures and can work at their own speed. Still pictures may also stimulate students to exercise their own powers of observation and expression. Since still pictures are so abundant in many sport and popular magazines they are an excellent way to involve students or groups of students in different types of projects. Another type of still picture that can be used to supplement instruction are sequence pictures, probably best produced by the sequence camera that takes eight sequence pictures at a manually adjusted speed and processes the prints in about thirty seconds.

Graphs can be used in determining relationships between factors of physical performance, e.g., students' achievement on physical fitness tests compared with the national or state average. Graphs may also be used to show the relationship between the depth of the knee bend and jumping height or the effect of knee extension upon distance kicking in football. It is a good technique if the teacher involves class participation and cooperation in developing graph relationships.

Diagrams are simplified drawings which usually depict fundamental plays or drills. Prime examples of the use of diagrams are found in teaching basketball, football, soccer, etc. Plays are diagrammed by using symbols for players and lines or paths for direction. Diagrams may also be used to show court markings, specific equipment used, and areas of responsibility. Pictures for a slide series may be used with diagrams to give realism to the presentation.

Bulletin Board, Chalkboard, Flannel Board, and Magnetic Board Techniques

The most effective use of pictures, charts, and diagrams depends on where and how they are put up. If they are shown on a bulletin board they should be placed at the eye level of the students who will see it. Generally an eight by four-foot bulletin board is a good all-purpose board. It should be placed in a well-lighted area and as far as possible out of the way of showers and dressing area. Generally a good place for a bulletin board is where students spend some time waiting. Materials should not be left on the bulletin board for an extended length of time for they tend to lose their effectiveness.

The chalkboard is probably the most frequently used and readily available visual aid in physical education. Chalkboards are most frequently used in teaching team activities. Small chalkboards imprinted with permanent basketball court or football playing positions make visualization easier. Some clipboard-size chalkboards come with aluminum chalk pens. More elaborate playboards come in sizes up to four feet by five feet and do not use chalk. On some boards, standard formations are marked with semipermanent markers while player movement is indicated with water color markers that can be removed with damp cloth. The semipermanent marks may also be removed with a cleaning solvent. Recently, magnetic boards and felt boards have been used but probably never will replace the chalkboard due to its versatility.

Tape Recorder, Cassette, and Record Player Techniques

Sound effects and music often enhance the learning situation by providing additional motivation to the students. Certain classes, such as folk, square, and modern dance classes could not function without music from tape recorders, cassettes, or record players. Audio techniques have been used successfully in movement education, calisthenics, free expression, gymnastics, etc. Many routines in physical education are enhanced by the use of tape recorders, cassettes, and record players.

Motion Picture Techniques

Traditionally, the most widely used audio-visual technique is the use of motion picture films, which are easily available in all types of activities. The use of motion pictures may give rise to several problems, but the teacher who plans adequately will avoid most of them. A good teacher will always preview a motion picture film before showing it to the class. By studying the film beforehand, specific points may be indicated during the film and desired objectives reached. Problems with motion pictures may include the cost or advance arrangement for film rentals, arrangement for projectors, and operation of the equipment. It is usually a good practice to have student operators of projectors when possible so that the teacher is free to indicate key points. The technique of using a *cordless pointer* permits the instructor to point out details of the projected picture from any spot in the room by means of a point of bright light. The use of an *athletic analyzer projector* allows film to be run at various speeds and to back up and show a rerun as many times as necessary to illustrate a point.

Loop Film Techniques

The 8-mm loop film has many advantages when used as a teaching technique. The 8-mm cartridge generally contains from three to five minutes of film. It requires no threading and will run continuously, enabling students to watch a skill demonstrated until it is understood. Eight-mm and super-eight cartridge projectors allow for maximum ease of portability and may be set up anywhere in relatively small space. This technique enables students to view the cartridge loop films anytime during the instructional period, and enables them to have a greater control over their learning experience, which is an essential step toward individualization.

Figure 1
Loop film projector and cartridge

35-mm Slide and Filmstrip Techniques

The two-by-two slide projector and the 35-mm slide is probably one of the most inexpensive visual techniques available to the classroom teacher. One does not have to use an expensive camera to make acceptable slides, particularly outdoors. Any beginning cameraman can use the automatic-eye camera, since there is nothing to do except to frame the object in the viewfinder and shoot. This makes it particularly acceptable for any teacher. In addition, hundreds of slides may be stored in a tray or drawer, taking up very small space. The film-strip is very similar to the slides, except that a 35-mm camera must be used. The filmstrip is simply a series of slides connected together. A big advantage in using slides and filmstrips over moving film in teaching is that the teacher can set the pace for using them. Certain frames may require longer viewing and discussion than others. There is also much more flexibility in that one may back up, skip frames or slides, or take each picture as it comes in sequential order. Filmstrips may be used by one pupil as well as for class presentation. This is ideal for the individualization process in teaching and learning.

Teachers may use a written or recorded script with 35-mm slides and film-strips to explain in detail various skill activities step by step. This technique is invaluable in impressing upon students the fundamental teaching points.

Overhead Projector Techniques

The overhead projector is one piece of audio-visual equipment that has almost completely revolutionized today's teaching techniques. This piece of equipment has many advantages for the teacher: It comes in a compact and lightweight model, it is simple to operate, it can be used in the front of the room, and it lends itself to good teaching techniques. The visual information to be projected is contained on transparent material placed on the flat lens-top surface of the projector. A bright lamp located beneath the stage transmits light through a transparency into a mirror and lens system located directly over the center of the lens top and from there the image is projected onto the screen. Because the transparency is relatively large, it is fully visible in a normally lighted classroom. The placement of the projector and the image make overhead projection especially convenient for the teacher to face the class while using this technique. From this position, the teacher can talk directly to students while pointing out special aspects of the visual, changing transparencies, or even adding information by writing on the transparency with a water-soluble, colored, or opaque marking pen.

The overhead projector may be used in teaching various skill activities. Since the unit is portable, it may be moved with little difficulty, and its ease of operation lends itself to student use. It has the same advantages and implications for use as cartridge projectors, 35-mm slides, and filmstrips. Transparencies may either be bought commercially or be made by the teacher. Thermofax machines can reproduce drawings onto transparencies for use on the overhead projector.

Videotape Techniques

Instructional television has been used by physical education instructors in teaching various activities, and it has been found that by itself, no matter how good it is, it cannot replace a teacher who interacts with students in real-life situations. It has underscored, however, the necessity for lesson planning, cooperation between the television teacher and the classroom teacher, development of goals, and the use of other good teaching techniques. In order for physical education to gain most from instructional television, much work and thought must be expended. Techniques that work well in the gymnasium do not always lead to successful teaching on television. Students may be assigned to watch the "game of the week" in order to learn the basic rules, strategy, etc., of the activity being covered. These observations might end in class presentation, discussion, etc.

The increasing use of the portable videotape recorder and camera is opening up another aspect of classroom television. Pictures can be originated on the spot and recorded for immediate or delayed playback. The portable videotape recorder is adaptable to almost any activity in physical education where students may be taped performing specific skills in order to correct faults, teams may be taped in order to evaluate playing strategy, and even the general class procedure may be taped to provide feedback for the teacher in the form of instructional weak points and trouble spots. Generally, it is advisable for a student or another faculty member to perform the videotaping. It must be stressed that time for evaluation for all concerned must be taken when viewing videotape. Videotape is an invaluable tool in recognizing faults and good points when adequate time is spent critically reviewing the tape.

Resource Center Techniques

Because physical education is taking on a new look across the country due to a change in philosophy toward a more individualized approach, much emphasis is placed on the student's awareness of the need and ability to seek out needed assistance in learning any particular skill or knowledge. The student is directed through the course content by an individual contract that enables him to avoid repetition of instruction and move at his own pace. To accomplish this new idea in physical education requires certain changes which have not been apparent in programs of the past. One of the most marked changes comes in the set up of facilities. No longer is the gymnasium required to be free for "full-court" basketball. Instead it takes on the appearance of a learning laboratory with stations featuring mechanical devices or whatever is necessary to accomplish the particular objectives of the activity. A room that is frequently "inactive" becomes a resource laboratory where a teacher is able to utilize the many audio-visual aids available to physical education.

This resource center comes in many sizes and shapes. The teacher by exerting some creative ability can set up a laboratory containing any number of the audio-visual aids available. The walls can be used to hold posters demonstrating skills or getting across information. The resource center should contain a library of *books, pamphlets, rules summaries,* and *related readings* on the students' level for their use in seeking additional information on history, skills, instruction, ways to improve skills, and any area needed regarding the activity being taught. This library should also have books and articles of interest involving professionals or outstanding achievers in sports. Many students have a keen interest in sports but may not have had an opportunity to pursue their interests.

The resource center may also be an area where students can use loop films, movies, slides, filmstrips, and records that have been produced to show skills broken down and demonstrated by experts. Through the use of the films, the student may observe correct skill techniques, examine game situations, and gain an understanding of the basis of his instruction at a particular level. Loop films and filmstrips are becoming readily available to schools through the media center and through the loan program.

A rather new addition to the resource center is the cassette television. These cassettes come in a variety of sports activities and are not only excellent for teaching skills but they are easy to operate and maintain. Other aids which are of value in a resource center are chalkboards, bulletin boards, screens, record players, tape recorders, overhead projectors, and videotape recorders and projectors. Loop film projectors and film cartridges may be used unsupervised in the resource center where students may select the cartridge describing the skill or concept needed and view it in the six to eight minutes required.

MECHANICAL TECHNIQUES

A valuable asset to the teacher of physical education in teaching physical education activities has been the adaptation and use of many mechanical devices that have been constructed to utilize and make the instruction of a particular skill more efficient. Mechanical devices vary from the homemade variety to expensive versions manufactured by companies featuring sports equipment. Only an example of the mechanical devices available will be described here for several physical education activities.

Archery

Archery is a skill that has a variety of mechanical devices available that will help the student improve shooting skills. These range from simple *nock locators* to complex *range-finder sights.* The nock locator was designed to improve shooting ability. Several varieties are available but all help to locate the exact point on the bow string where the arrow should be nocked each time to provide the same level of release.

Stabilizers are devices which attach to the front of the bow and provide the student with the ability to maintain a steadier draw prior to release. A necessary aid for any archery student is the *bow stringer*. This device is a piece of cord which fits over both ends of the bow and is used to bend the bow while the string is placed in position.

The part of the bow which the arrow rests upon is called the rest, and several devices can be used on the rest to provide last-second stability to the arrow upon release. A *flipper rest* keeps the arrow from as much lateral deviation near the fletching upon release. *String releases, finger protectors,* and *shooting gloves* are necessary in one form or another to keep the student from experiencing discomfort while maintaining a full draw position prior to release.

Sights, scopes, and *range finders* are available but will probably be outside the scope of classroom instruction. These devices help the shooter to locate the target and sight-in at the proper spot for greater accuracy. The *four-pound bow* is used by beginning archers at close range to get the correct shooting position.

Sometimes an archer will experience difficulty in determining the exact location of the grip position. If the grip changes, the arrow flight changes. To avoid an inconsistent flight pattern a *set grip position* is used. To help locate the same position each time an archer can use a homemade or commercial locator. The commercial locator is a leather ridge attached to the grip section of the bow. The archer feels the ridge in the same spot of his hand every time he begins to draw. The homemade locator is a method of aligning two lines, one on the bow with one on the hand. A piece of one-eighth-inch tape is placed on the grip on or near the pivot point with another piece of tape placed on the hand so that the two tapes line up when the archer is in a good grip position.

Just as every archer has check points on his face during the anchor position, some archers have *body checks* with the string as it is drawn to the chest area. Body structure and shooting style determine whether or not an archer will have a body check or contact point on his body with the string. Most archers who do have a body check wear a shirt protector that is usually made of plastic or leather. The protector keeps the string from catching on the clothing which may send the arrow low and left of the target.

The *draw-check device* is any accessory that notifies the archer that his arrow has reached the full draw position. In learning to perform a draw check the beginning archer does a visual check on the position of the tip of the arrow. If this method does not prove accurate enough or the archer has difficulty in performing the skill correctly because of body structure, any commercial draw-check device may be used. The most popular is called a *clicker* and is based on an audio signal delivered when the tip of the arrow comes past the strip (the metal snaps down to make a clicking sound). The archer does not need to look at the tip of the arrow if it is properly set.

In teaching archery to large groups either indoors or outdoors, it has been found beneficial to make use of the *archer backstop nets* to catch arrows and help prevent breakage and give additional safety. The nets are made of a heavy-gauge nylon netting for indoor use, and the archer cage is often used with multiple-side backstops which can be set up on the side of an area where other activities are taking place (see Figure 2 on page 26).

Badminton

There are many mechanical devices that are useful in teaching badminton skills. *Footprint guides* may be used for helping to locate the correct positioning of the feet during play. They are usually cutouts of feet marked on the floor. A *Peteka ball* may be used by beginners to learn to hit the bird. The Peteka ball is a very large badminton bird usually of a very soft material. *Lines* may be marked on a backwall to facilitate placement of the bird. In order to overcome fundamental difficulties, *shorter racquets* may be used in limited space. *Grip prints,* showing position of the hand on the racquet, and *wrist positioners* and *stabilizers* may also be useful. *Taped-off areas* may be used to increase accuracy on the part of the learner. Placing the shuttle in a specific area time after time will improve playing ability. A *rope* may be used for a player to practice hitting the shuttle a specific height, while at the same time trying to place the shuttle in a designated area. This device is sometimes used to perfect the deep clear shot.

Figure 2
Archer backstop nets and archer cage

Basketball

The most common mechanical device used in learning basketball is to tape an X on the backboard as a *target* for students shooting layups. With this technique, younger students can "aim" the ball for the spot while learning a very basic skill. Also used with younger students is the *Little League basketball adapter,* a device that is a separate goal and backboard which is attached to the regulation goal and lowers the goal height from the regulation ten feet to just eight and one-half feet. At the same time it projects two feet closer to the foul line.

Another shooting device used in basketball for getting students to aim for the rim of the goal is a *regulation rim,* ten feet high with no backboard, mounted on a pole with wheels so that it can be easily transported. Since there is no backboard, students may shoot from a full 360 degrees and increase accuracy in shooting without the visual cue of the backboard from which to bank. This device is very useful in large classes or where there are few goals in a gymnasium.

Some studies have reported the benefit of practicing with an *oversized basketball* for improving shooting ability. The ball is 31 inches in circumference compared to the regular size of 29¾ inches and weighs 22.5 ounces compared to the regular weight of 20.5 ounces. This ball has been found beneficial in teaching rebounding, developing hand-grip strength for ball control, and as a motivational factor in increasing the vertical jump.

Metal inner rims that are inserted into the regular basketball rims have been used to increase accuracy in shooting and to develop rebounding ability. The metal inner rim is large enough for a regular basketball to go through but smaller than the inside of a regular basketball rim.

Rebounding devices used in basketball may be found commercially or be homemade. Homemade rebounders include putting *tape, boards,* or *rope* across the goal so that the ball will not go through but will rebound. Commercial devices include the *Reboundome* constructed of transparent acrylic which gives a unique ball deflection surface.

Figure 3
Reboundome

McCall's Rebounder is another commercial rebounder that attempts to achieve a training effect by causing the player to use above normal strength in rebounding the ball. This rebounder consists of a closed basket on a high pole and chute with an arm on which the ball that is rebounded rests.

Another device which attempts to achieve the same effect may be home-made. It is composed of a *webbing nest* for a regulation basketball. The nest is connected to a five-sixteenth-inch elastic cord by means of a swivel snap, and has a thirty-five-foot rope. It can be set to any height, and with ample amount of rope, may even be hung on a gymnasium cross beam in the ceiling. The player has to jump to reach the ball, and when he grabs it and starts to pull the ball down, the elastic cord gives a certain degree of resistance, improving rebound grip strength of players.

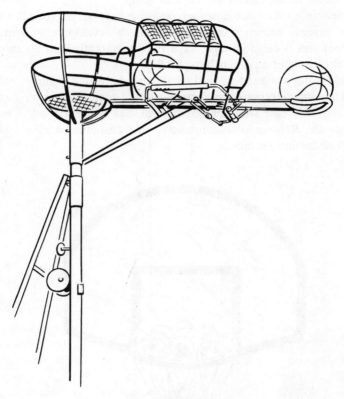

Figure 4
McCall's Rebounder

In basketball it is essential that players keep their eyes on the man guarding them, not on the ball. Perhaps the best-known teaching technique for improving dribbling are the *half-glasses* which produce a blinder against seeing the basketball while dribbling but do not hinder shooting vision. The device is made of plastic with an elastic strap and rubber-tipped edges. Other mechanical devices that may be used with blinders are standard physical education *cones* or *pylons* used for dribbling practice.

Another more sophisticated device for improving agility and reaction time is the *reactor,* a steel box 30″ × 30″ with four signal arrows and three signal lights. It is equipped with a steel tubular stand that adjusts from two to five feet in height. This device can be used in any sport, indoors or out, to develop agility, mobility, speed, and quickness. It can be programmed for seven possible commands by depressing push-button switches.

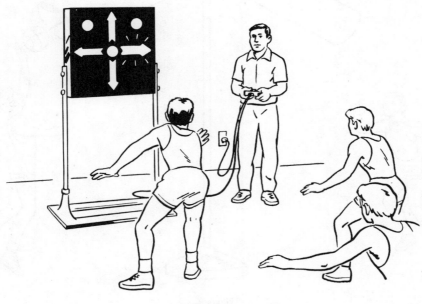

Figure 5
Reactor

Another teaching technique which may be used to develop agility, jumping ability, timing, and stamina is a *chute for two-man basketball*. It is suggested that this training device be used as a station in a circuit-training situation or as a warm-up procedure for basketball physical education classes or varsity work-outs. The game is conducted by first serving the ball through the chute and then tipping it back and forth through the chute until one player loses control. Because of the chute's construction, more than one jump is often required to tip the ball to the opposite side. The device can be adjusted either up or down to fit the needs of the individual participants.

Other devices used in teaching techniques include *weighted jackets* or *weighted innersoles* worn during stop-and-go drills, wind-sprints, or running up and down the stands for improving strength in the trunk and legs.

Bowling

There are several mechanical techniques used in teaching bowling. The most common technique is the *blinder*. This technique is devised to force a player to concentrate on aiming the ball at a spot on the floor rather than directly

Figure 6
Chute for two-man basketball

at the pins. A *bowling glove* may help a student improve his score by obtaining a more comfortable grip. *Taped-off areas* behind the foul line is a technique sometimes used to aid a student in improving the approach. *Towels* may be placed across the foul line to keep those students from fouling who have a habit of continually crossing the foul line. *Bowling machines* may be *altered* so that a certain spare or group of pins may be practiced continuously.

Dance

The most commonly used technique in teaching dance is *footprints* which are drawn or taped on the floor. Depending on the age group of the students, it is sometimes advantageous to use a variety of colors for the footprints. By using these, the students can more readily visualize the path their feet are to follow. Modern dance teachers often utilize *mirrors* and *stall bars* to help students perceive their movements, and develop flexibility.

Football

One of the techniques used in teaching backs to run with their knees high is the *tire run,* consisting of pairs of worn-out tires arranged in a long line. Players will run through the tires trying to avoid touching them, forcing their knees high and developing good running form. The *rope run* is also a device that may be used in teaching backs to run with their knees high. This is a device that consists of rope in a checkerboard arrangement with two lanes of squares. This same type of device may be created by laying stand-up *blocking dummies* on the ground spaced so that there is room to step between them. They may be spaced in such a fashion as to form an obstacle course for developing quickness as well as agility and balance. Blocking dummies, both the stand-up type and the hand type are very versatile. They may be used in a number of ways other than exclusively for blocking drills. *Blocking sleds,* both *two-man* and *seven-man,* are useful in teaching the techniques of blocking both for backs and linemen.

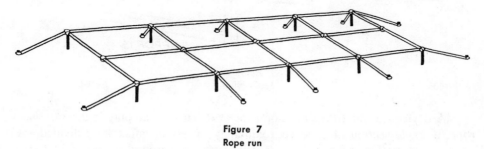

Figure 7
Rope run

The *reaction sled* consists of two movable side plates, a stationary center plate, and a movable stimulus mounted on a stationary base. The movable plates are pushed back and spring loaded. By hitting a trigger device with the stimuli, the plate moves forward. The student reacts to the movement of the stimuli and hits the plate that is triggered by the stimuli. A forceful blow is required to put the plate back to the starting position.

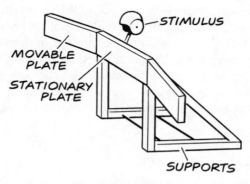

Figure 8
Reaction sled

A device used primarily for developing power in backs is the *Smitty Blaster*. This device has movable arms that are constructed so that a great deal of force is required to move them. A back runs through these arms at the proper angle with enough force to open them or he is pushed back. This device helps backs to hang onto the ball as well as achieve the proper running angle with powerful leg action.

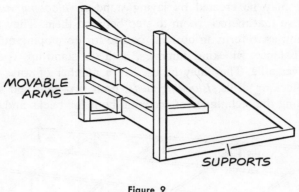

MOVABLE ARMS

SUPPORTS

Figure 9
Smitty Blaster

A device specific to the development of defensive line play is the *stationary rope*, a single section of rope approximately twenty-one feet long divided into seven equal sections by metal stakes driven into the ground to firmly anchor it. The defensive man assumes a defensive stance with his hands gripping the rope. An offensive man lines up opposite him and fires out on signal. The defensive man delivers a blow with his forearm on the blocker, but must maintain his grip with one hand. If the defensive man raises up, his grip is broken. This technique helps teach the defensive lineman to stay low and deliver a blow to the blocker.

A *pass-catching net* is a time-saving device. It may be tied beneath the crossbar of the goalpost to the two side poles. When quarterbacks, backs, and ends practice throwing and catching, this device may be used as a backup, stopping missed passes. *Narrow goalposts* are useful in developing accuracy for place kickers. They compel the kicker to work on accuracy as well as on distance in kicking. *Flag belts* (strips of canvas or plastic with stick-on patches on canvas belts buckled around players) are useful devices in teaching flag football. Flag belts come in various colors so that competing teams have different-colored flags.

Golf

There are several mechanical techniques that may be used in teaching golf. A *frame* for teaching the plane of the swing for all full shots using woods or irons may be constructed. The frame consists of two rectangular canvas-covered frames attached to each other at the top by fairly heavy hinges so that the angle of the two surfaces may be adjusted to fit the size of the individual and the length of the club being used. The canvas covering the center area of one of the inclined frames would be cut out so that a hole about three feet in diameter is formed. When in use, the two surfaces are spread out in the form of an inverted "V." The stance the player assumes is such that the upper portion of the body projects through the hole. When not in use the frame may be folded and stored against a wall.

Practice cages may also be made. A rectangular frame is first constructed equal to the desired length and width of the cage. The measurements can be as small as 10′ × 12′ if the practice area is small. Along the top of the frame is attached a piece of fairly fine but durable netting. The sides of the frame are covered with a fairly heavy grade of canvas. Another piece of canvas is attached to the frame to form the back of the cage. The canvas should be nailed on in such a way that there is approximately a one-foot overlap at the two far corners to prevent golf balls from going through when hit. A loose piece of canvas should be hung inside the cage about one and one-half feet in front of the rear canvas to help absorb the force of the ball.

A *driving mat* may be used with *plastic balls* or *cotton balls* indoors or with *soft rubber balls* outdoors. This teaching device is used by many golf teachers on rainy days. A *putting mat* can also be made from a piece of plywood on which carpeting is tacked. The cup may be put anywhere on the mat. A raised border around the far edge is helpful in keeping balls from rolling around the room after each putt.

A teaching technique for improving short approach shots is a series of *concentric circles*. The circles may be drawn or painted on the floor or on the wall. Another technique that is used to help keep the eyes on the ball is a *stick* about a foot long with a mouthpiece on one end. During the swing the mouthpiece is placed in the mouth to hold the stick, and the stick is aimed at the ball during the stroke.

The *Saf-Space Golf Ball* is a technique that may help students make correct contact with the golf ball. A one-quarter-inch hole is drilled through the center of a regulation rubber-centered golf ball. One end of a thirty-foot nylon cord three-sixteenths of an inch in diameter is attached to a 1¼ pound weight and the other end is inserted through the hole of the golf ball and knotted. By drawing lines on the floor and placing the weight on the center line, the instructor and student can see whether the student makes correct contact with the ball.

In teaching the correct grip a technique that is used many times is the use of a *modified golf club* with indentations in the grip so that it is almost impossible to assume an incorrect grip.

The *Golf-O-Tron* uses a modified missile-tracking computer and couples this with color photography of a selected golf course. Regulation clubs and golf balls are used, and exact yardage the ball will travel and the approximate position on the fairway is instantly shown after each shot. Each unit includes the computer, control blocks, microphone pickup, photo—electric-eye system, switch

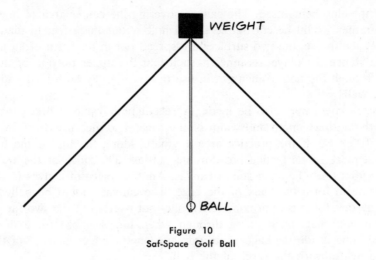

Figure 10
Saf-Space Golf Ball

system, display light system, nylon netting, projector, and golf course slide set, console with controls, carpeting for putting area, and wooden platform for tee area and calibrater. The overall dimensions are 15′ wide by 20′ deep with a ceiling of 10′ 6″.

The *Golf-Lite* may be used as a teaching technique in golf. It is a small light mounted on the shaft of a club and powered by a six-volt dry cell battery. Through a special lens arrangement, a fairly bright spot about the diameter of a dime is made visible on the floor or ground. As the club is swung, the eyes see an arc of light reflecting from the hitting surface through the hitting zone.

Gymnastics

Several teaching techniques are used in gymnastics to aid students in gaining confidence and prevent fear of falling. *Spotting belts* allow a performer to go through difficult moves without fear of falling and are especially useful for beginning students. Large *inner tubes* and *nets* filled with foam rubber are especially helpful in beginning classes to avoid injury and increase confidence. Sometimes a revolving *pedestal* or a *bongo board* is used to help students develop a better sense of kinesthetic perception or balance.

Tumbling belts, lunge belts, head protectors, safety straps for parallel bars, *handgrips, twisting belts, traveling suspension systems,* and *overhead spotting rigs* are all devices used to decrease the possibility of injury.

The various types of belts fit around the student's body and are either attached to supports or held by two other students. They are used to prevent the student from falling to the floor in case the exercise is not completed in the proper form.

Handgrips, made of lampwick or leather, help the student maintain a high coefficient of friction and at the same time protect the hand while performing on apparatus. The *traveling suspension system* and the *overhead spotting rig* are both devices that use guy ropes and wires in conjunction with a belt to help the student perform certain activities but at the same time prevent falling.

Handball

Handball requires excellent hand and eye coordination which compels teachers to devise methods to improve this aspect. One teaching technique used by teachers of handball is the use of an adjustable *tee* upon which the ball is placed and struck by the player. This works on the same principle as the batting tee in baseball and is primarily used for beginners.

Figure 11
Handball tee

Beginners may have success early in handball by using a *tennis ball* or a *larger ball*. The larger ball should rebound from the front wall with less velocity and will provide a larger target.

The *Exergenie* is used to strengthen the side arm and overarm stroke. It is a device that allows a person to dial the amount of tension needed for the pull. Increasing the tension slightly as strength increases allows students to progress at their own rate.

To improve accuracy in handball a teacher may place a *strip of tape* on the front wall about eighteen inches above the floor for students to keep all returns at or below the tape. Sometimes *targets* are placed on the front wall to aid students in improving aim at a particular spot.

Soccer-Speedball

Since the main components of soccer-speedball are considered to be balance, agility, and power, the mechanical devices used in instruction may be designed to improve these qualities. Many of the devices used in football are useful in teaching soccer-speedball. For example, *blocking dummies* may be used to create an obstacle course. A ball is used while going through the course in order to improve ball handling with the feet. The *rope run* could be adapted for use by increasing the distance between hurdles and raising the ropes to a height that permits the ball to roll under the ropes. Students hurdle the ropes and control the ball between hurdles.

In heading the ball in soccer or speedball, one of the main objectives is directing the ball where the player wants it to go. It is with this objective that *soccer-speedball tetherball* can help. The idea is to play tetherball between two individuals, specifying that the only way to hit the ball legally is to head it. Not only is this device beneficial in improving reaction and timing, but also it eliminates the chore of chasing the ball that is so common during heading drills.

In learning controlled kicking, an apparatus of *elastic ropes* that is commonly used in football agility drills and pylons is used. The ropes are high enough off the ground to allow a soccer ball to roll under them. The object is to move a soccer ball on the ground around the pylons while at the same time avoiding stepping on the ropes.

To develop power kicking, a *spring-loaded medicine ball* may be used. The player kicks the ball with the traditional soccer kick, and if he has followed through correctly, the ball will miss his stationary foot on its recoil. This device is used only by soccer-speedball players who have developed average strength and ability in their kicking.

A device that may be used in drills for both football and soccer-speedball is the *kicker's bullpen*. The kicker's bullpen is made of a metal frame covered by a small rope mesh netting. The kicker kicks the ball into the open area at the front of the device. This enables a strong kick with a minimum of time loss in retrieving the ball. A similar device is the *ballboy rebound net*. The ball may be kicked or thrown into the net and easily retrieved. Still another soccer-speedball device is the *narrow goal*. The principle behind this is much the same as that of the narrow goal used in football. Accuracy is the primary skill developed.

A *target goal* emphasizes both accuracy and ball placement. This device can be made with relative ease and small expense. The device is constructed using a large sheet of plywood, with several three-inch diameter holes cut in the sheet. A light is mounted in each hole and connected to a master switch. Each light is controlled independently of the others. The board is set upright representing the mouth of a goal. It must be braced securely. The student dribbles the ball downfield, watching the board. As one of the lights flashes, the student kicks the ball and tries to hit the light. The lights represent the open area of the

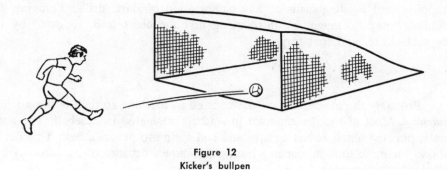

Figure 12
Kicker's bullpen

goal when a goalie is present. The board may be covered with a force absorber in order to minimize the rebound.

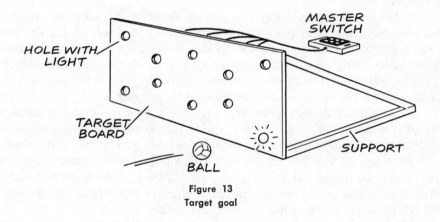

MASTER
SWITCH

HOLE WITH
LIGHT

TARGET
BOARD

BALL

SUPPORT

Figure 13
Target goal

Another mechanical device used in soccer which may be used in the development of kicking and heading skill as well as in game situations, is a *rebound board*. The board is identical in principle to the ones used in tennis, although its construction is different. Ideally, the board should be the size of a soccer goal, although it may be smaller. One-half-inch planks are nailed to a frame and reinforced from behind with 2″ × 4″ or 2″ × 6″ studding. The board can be used in a wide range of drills, is portable, and is rather inexpensive to construct. In the upright position the rebound board is an excellent backstop for kicking drills. In the inclined position the rebound board provides the greatest number of really unique and varied teaching situations. When slanted at about 45° the board rebounds a kicked ball into the air, the trajectory depending upon the speed of the ball and the angle of impact upon the board. A ball rebounded into the air introduces a completely new dimension in the teaching of kicking, trapping, and heading drills or any combination of these drills. Trapping, for example, may be taught by introducing first the chest trap, followed by the stomach, knee, and foot traps.

Softball

Probably the most common device used in teaching softball is the *pitching machine*. Most of the devices used in softball originated in baseball. The automatic pitching machine has an arm and coil spring to propel a ball. This device allows for more time in teaching hitting techniques because of its accuracy and regularity in throwing.

A *batting tee* is another device used in softball for teaching hitting. The batting tee consists of an expandable metal rod from a support base with a rubber pedestal. The batting tee is used to develop hand and eye coordination, to help players concentrate on leveling their swing, and in general to aid in developing hitting techniques.

A *hitting net* allows a player to perfect his swing if a large playing area is not available. This technique gives the same feeling as a softball bat except that a small net, approximately 12″ × 6″ in size, is designed to catch a pitched ball. If the batter swings at the ball properly, he will be able to catch the ball in the net. This technique is designed to improve the batting eye and timing of a batter when use of a bat is not feasible because of the playing area.

A weighted ball that is the same size as a regular softball is often used except it is heavier in weight than a regular ball. Using this technique will tend to develop throwing strength and produce a psychological effect in throwing.

An *isometric ball* is a regular ball with a large hook inserted deep enough that it can't be pulled out with elastic rope attached to the hook and tied to a fixed object. The use of this ball develops strength and allows for strength development in actual throwing position and action.

The *isometric bat* is a regular bat with a large hook inserted in the hitting area attached to a hook and a fixed object. This bat allows for developing strength in actual hitting position and action.

Batting cages are also used in developing hitting skill. Batting cages are large areas screened in nylon net to catch the batted ball. This allows for indoor hitting practice and saves time in retrieving balls.

Swimming

In swimming there are many teaching techniques that may be used which involve mechanical devices. *Kick-boards* are used to isolate the legs in learning the skill of kicking. *Pull buoys* are placed between the legs to keep the lower body up in the water while working on the movement of the arm stroke. *Inner tubes* may be used to help support the legs in teaching correct arm strokes. *Arm floats, waist floats, ring* or *buoy floats,* and *barbell floats* are used to support the body above the surface so that beginners may work on various aspects of the swimming stroke.

A *mirror* placed at the end of the pool may be used as a technique to allow the swimmer to see himself as he swims. *Hand paddles* are used to help the hands move through the strokes correctly. A *pace clock* may be used to let the swimmer tell how long it took him to swim a certain distance and thus develop a steady pace. *Resistance exercise machines* with padded slanted bench and ropes attached to overhanging pulleys and weights may be used to develop strength in the shoulders and arms in pulling.

Tennis

In tennis, as with many other skill activities, the development of fundamental skills is essential if the student is to gain success and enjoyment from further instruction and playing time. Various mechanical tennis devices have been developed to help the physical education teacher eliminate the more common fundamental errors. Most of the following mechanical devices can be constructed by the teacher with limited facilities and budget.

In younger students, the size of the standard tennis racquet is a detriment because of its relatively long length and heavy weight. This problem may be largely overcome if commercially made racquets or *shortened tennis racquets* are made available. In addition to the obvious advantage of greater maneuverability, these shorter racquets are also useful in limited space areas and are inexpensive. If shortened racquets are not available, wooden paddles like the type used in deck or paddle tennis may be used in much the same way.

One problem that is often encountered by beginning tennis players is assuming the correct grip each time the racquet is gripped. One simple device to supplement grip instruction is to outline with waterproof paint, the *grip positions* for the forehand and backhand. It is also advisable to use a different color of paint for each grip. The hand outline may be obtained by chalking the hand gripping the racquet in the desired position. This device is particularly beneficial in large classes in that the marked racquet may be rotated to numerous students and thus time is cut down for individual inspection.

Another crucial fundamental point in beginning tennis is the position of the racquet head in relation to the arm and wrist. Instruction in this area may be supplemented by utilizing a *wrist positioner*. This device consists of an elastic cord that is tied to the racquet head and also to the individual's wrist. A *wrist stabilizer* may be used in conjunction with this device. A very effective and inexpensive wrist stabilizer may be constructed by simply taping or strapping a shoehorn to the front and back of the wrist. This aids in restricting movement in executing forehand and backhand drives. The third point at which the position of the racquet, wrist, and arm become misaligned is the elbow. An *elbow restrictor* can be made very easily with a cardboard milk container with the ends cut off. The milk container is placed over the elbow, thereby restricting elbow flexion. Although this device may be somewhat painful, it does encourage proper arm action when executing the backhand stroke.

Hitting the ball with the edge of the racquet is one primary headache of beginning students and their instructors. Accuracy in stroking the ball is almost impossible without mastering this fundamental technique. There are several devices which allow the student to acquire the feel for the "sweet spot" of the racquet. One device which is helpful in this respect is the use of partially strung racquets with a square cut out in the center of each racquet. It provides instant feedback on the success of the student to find the "sweet spot" because to be a good hit, the ball must go through the empty square. This device is best used when executing a ground stroke by the self-toss method or in practicing the serve. The device serves a double purpose in that normally unusable racquets are once more utilized. A "bull's-eye" may be constructed on a racquet by weaving a piece of clothesline through the strings in a circular manner, leaving a six-inch diameter circle in the center of the strings. This device seems to offer fewer advantages in that it is difficult to tell exactly where the ball hit the racquet when performing individually, and more time is probably spent in preparing the racquets for use.

The second area of interest with regard to mechanical devices in tennis is in the development of a smoothly coordinated stroke. By using elastic shock cord there are several stroke developers that can be made inexpensively and without much preparation time. In teaching the forehand and backhand strokes, a *vertical elastic stroke developer* may be used with a great deal of success.

For practice in hitting the serve and other overhead shots, a *horizontal elastic stroke developer* may be used. The horizontal serving device is similar

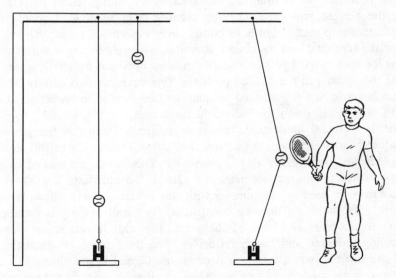

Figure 14
Elastic shock cord

to the stroke developer and is used in much the same way. Not difficult to construct, it consists of the ball-and-cord unit of the stroke developer and an additional piece of rope or cord tied to the free end of the shock cord.

The *serving unit* may be placed in the corners of the tennis court, high enough so that the ball will be hit with the arm and racquet fully extended. The ends of the rope are pulled through the fencing, far enough from the corner post so that there will be no danger of striking the fence on the follow-through. The free ends are extended and fastened to the fence with hooks. The ball may be raised or lowered from its original position by releasing one of the hooks and resetting it when the desired ball height has been determined. The serving unit may also be strung between two poles or used indoors by attaching hooks at desired positions in the corners and proceeding in a manner similar to that described for the fence. Net standards may also be used.

Another device in teaching the serve similar to the horizontal server unit is the *ballboy server,* which holds a tennis ball at exactly the right hitting height and position for each player and permits the player to practice the serve without encountering the added problem of the ball toss. The player gets the idea and the "feel" of hitting the ball solidly with the arm extended to full reach as in the serve itself. The slightest hit will release the ball for a completely normal flight into the opposite court without interference from either the racquet or the swing. The device is equally effective for ground strokes for it may be adjusted to any height and returns to the preset height after attaching the next ball.

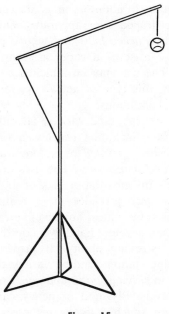

Figure 15
Ballboy server

Since many tennis courts are equipped with an area designed for practice hitting, the *backboard* is a very practical device since it is usually made of wood and has the advantage of being relatively inexpensive and durable. The backboard is simply a long section of wood or concrete against which the ball may be hit. The backboard should be long enough to accommodate eight or more players at one time and high enough to prevent balls from being hit over the top. The use of the backboard is so valuable in developing good strokes and good footwork that many teachers would rather have a backboard and fewer courts if a choice between the two had to be made.

Closely akin to wall instruction is the use of bounce-back nets. The *rebound net* has several distinct advantages over that of the wooden or concrete backboard. First, it eliminates the problem of noise, particularly if the backboard practice takes place indoors. Second, it makes for better timing of the ball in that it actually lengthens the rebound interval by seconds without reducing the ball's velocity. By adjusting the angle of tilt, all types of shots can be practiced: low drives, high bounding balls, overhead smash, volleys, etc. By changing the net tension, anywhere from slack to tight, the depth and velocity of rebound may be varied. In this manner the unit may be adjusted to the amount of space available as well as to the skill of each student. In addition, it has the added advantage of being so light that any two students can easily transport it.

For bad-weather or indoor instruction in stroke development, *tumbling mats* are beneficial in that they control and limit the rebound of the ball (which is essential in cramped areas), and also targets can be readily attached to them for accuracy and control work. In addition, mats are generally available and frequently stored on walls or draped over apparatus. Other suitable bad-weather tennis equipment may include *fleece balls* and *whiffle balls. Rope* or *string nets* may also be used—these consist of a rope or string of suitable length with paper or cloth streamers. The net may be attached to chairs or stands, and is easily portable. In addition, this type of net allows low-hit balls to pass under so that the game may be continuous.

In developing stroke accuracy and variety, all different types and descriptions of targets may be used, including *cardboard rings, hula hoops, bicycle inner tubes, inflated plastic toys, painted or chalked targets, bed sheets, wastebaskets, cardboard boxes, and tennis cans.* The uses of these various targets are only limited by the teacher's imagination or lack of it.

The *tethered rebound ball* provides more realistic practice when used across the net. It may be used on almost any level surface at school or at home. When used correctly, it can develop hand-eye coordination, timing, an early backswing, footwork, and stroking ability. It provides the teacher of large groups with another teaching station, lending variety to the program.

To improve accuracy in serving, *poles* and *cords* may be used to divide the area above the net into levels. Plywood or heavy cardboard planks one foot wide and eight feet high are attached to the net posts with the levels marked. The various levels and the shots corresponding to them should be stressed: level one—hard shots, cross court and passing shots; level two—rally and·

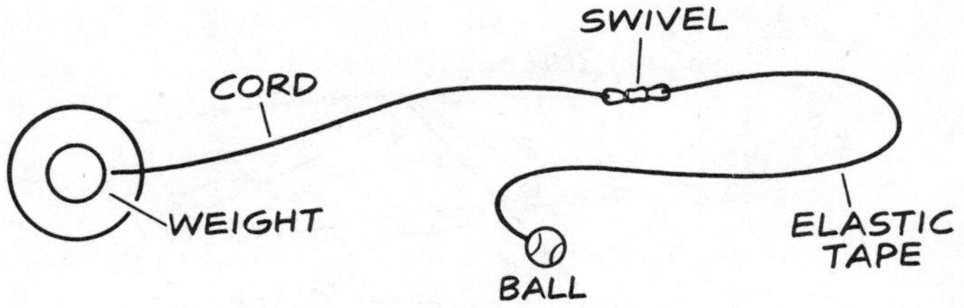

Figure 16
Tethered rebound ball

medium paced deep shots; level three—medium or slow speed when time is needed to recover for the next return; and level four—lobs, with the height of the lob depending on the nature of the lob, aggressive or defensive.

To aid in footwork, *cardboard* or *vinyl rings* may be utilized. These should be placed in areas where group and individual instruction will take place. Within these circles, the students may perform footwork drills (pivoting and stepping). In addition, these circles make excellent targets for developing stroke accuracy.

Nets or *canvas backdrops* as teaching devices accomplish two things: they provide a place into which the ball can be stroked without the problem of the ball rebounding, and several players can stroke a ball at one time without the danger of being hit. Moreover, backdrops are essential where usable wall space is at a minimum. The *backdrop* may be constructed of either a net or canvas material, and either may be attached to a wire in such a way that removal to one side of the gymnasium is a simple matter.

The *stroking bench* and *lane markings* are two more valuable devices used in the instruction of tennis skills. The player stands close enough to the bench so that in his natural swing the racquet will pass directly over the center of the bench. The instructor (or a pupil) drops the ball on the bench and the player swings at it as it rises from the bounce. To hit the ball straight ahead, the ball is tossed or dropped on line 1 and the racquet head should be brought parallel with line 1 at the moment of impact with the ball; i.e., player learns to follow the path of the line. To hit the ball to the right, the ball is dropped on line 2 and the racquet head travels along line 2. To hit the ball to the left, the ball is dropped on line 3 and the racquet head follows line 3.

A final mechanical device for tennis that will be covered in this section is the *Tennis Trainer* or *Ballboy*. The machine can hold over 100 balls without reloading, and since it has wheels and is covered, it can be used indoors or out. It can throw from behind the baseline to the opposite baseline, cross court, down lines, as well as angle shots and lobs. It also has variable speed controls.

Track and Field

Teaching techniques used in track are designed to enhance speed and quickness. Efforts have been made to improve race times by improving *starting blocks*. The conventional type of starting block consists of two movable foot pads

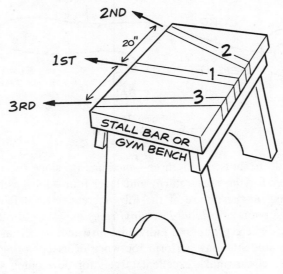

Figure 17
Stroking bench

mounted on a shaft. Metal spikes on both ends of the shaft secure the block to the track. The movable pads enable the runner to place his feet in the most advantageous position. Another type of starting block, the European-type block, consists of two separate pads that have spikes projecting from the bottom. There is no center shaft. Still another type of block is the standing type. This type supposedly utilizes certain mechanical principles in improving performance.

The *Decan Timing Device* is an instrument that may be used to improve reaction to the starting gun. It presents a stimulus and records reaction time. Through knowledge of the results, starting times may be improved through practice.

Pace lights may be installed around the track that blink on at any set pace so that the runner can tell the pace he is setting. If a runner is behind the pace, the light will blink on farther and farther ahead of him.

Success in relay races is dependent upon the ability to pass the baton. This is especially true in short-distance relay races. *Elongated batons* for practice are useful in improving exchange techniques. As the runners improve in skill, the batons are progressively shortened until they are regulation size.

Hurdling devices may be constructed with the same idea in mind. *Styrofoam hurdles* may be constructed in order to alleviate the pain involved in hitting a hurdle. These devices may be used until proficiency is attained and then replaced with regulation hurdles.

There are mechanical techniques that are useful in field events. Discus throwers have found that the use of *weight plates* is advantageous for warm-up. The plates are thrown with the same technique as the discus. This device is useful in improving performance. Shot-putters may use shots that are *lighter* to improve form and then *heavier* than the normal shot to facilitate warm-up and improve performance.

The Decan Timing Device may also be used to help improve quickness across the ring for both shot-putters and discus throwers. This is best accomplished by attaching the foot mats to the Decan Timer. The thrower or putter initiates the clock by removing one foot from the back mat and stops the clock by stepping on the mat at the front of the ring. By knowing speed of movement and by viewing movement with analytic visual aids, students may improve time.

The use of high quality *jumping pits* serves to gain the confidence of the jumper since the chance of injury is greatly lessened by landing in the pit. Consequently, the beginner becomes more willing to attempt greater heights. There are several types of pits from which to select, but the major criterion of selection should be the degree of safety that it will provide. The types available include foam sheets in mesh bags, plastic-covered foam, and the newer air-filled pits.

Volleyball

Volleyball also lends itself to the use of various instructional techniques. As in many sports, *target areas* may be set up for the volleyball class with court markings drawn on the floor on either side of the net. For example, in teaching the placement of the serve, a court may be divided into areas where students are able to self-test by practicing serving repeatedly into the various areas.

In teaching passing and set-ups, a teacher may stretch a *rope taut* across the gymnasium from one basket hoop to the other and have students volley the ball back and forth over the rope. This technique teaches the high set-up which is valuable in the progression of the spike skill. By varying the use of the rope, students can gain much benefit by learning proper placement of the ball.

A *chute* extending over the court from the bleachers may be used in dropping a volleyball to practice the set-up in volleyball. The ball rolls to the end of the chute and is contacted as it drops toward the floor.

The *tetherball prop* is a technique that is easily constructed and is very useful in many ways for teaching volleyball skills. This technique has the advantage of having the ball suspended in air, making it easier for the teacher to demonstrate correct ball-handling skills. Players may see for themselves the exact spot where the hands or arms should meet the ball and learn to jump upward with a two-foot takeoff, which is essential in getting maximum height prior to meeting the ball in the spike. To construct a tetherball prop for volleyball, remove the cord that is connected to the ball and pull a clothesline through the loop on the ball (a plastic line is best as it is narrower and tends to give a little with the contact of the ball). The tetherball prop may be used in several ways in volleyball:

1. Fasten each end of the rope securely to one end of each of two nine-foot poles (two people must support the poles in an upright position).
2. Poles may be used with base supports to suspend the ball. One pole may

Figure 18
Tetherball props

be tilted to allow for either a taut or slackened rope, depending upon the skill being taught.

3. One end of the rope may be tied to a net standard at the side of the court or tied to a basketball rim at the end of the basketball court.

Wrestling

Wrestling has few mechanical techniques but uses several training methods employed by other sports. *Distance running* and *weight training* probably lead the list. *Weight machines, isometric devices, Exergenie* and *isokinetic machines* are used to develop strength.

Horizontal and *vertical lines* may be drawn on the floor and wall of the wrestling room for determining distance covered in a given move. The rectangles should measure 1' × 2½'. The horizontal lines on the wall will show headline and waistline upward and downward motion. Vertical lines will assist in calculating the distance moved by a wrestler. The teacher should stand at the side when analyzing a wrestler's position.

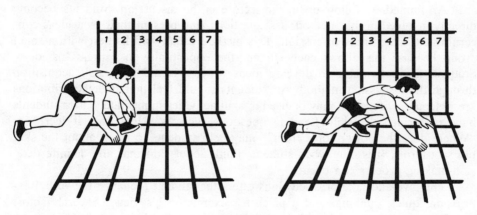

Figure 19
Horizontal and vertical lines

METHODS USED IN TEACHING PHYSICAL EDUCATION

Methods are combinations of techniques that are organized into some pattern and are primarily concerned with how subject matter is presented.

Lecture Method

The lecture method is probably more widely used in theory classes than in skill classes but it can be equally useful in both. Lecture, consisting of oral communication on the part of the teacher, is an extremely important method of instruction. Beginner's classes can probably benefit from initial sessions that cover rules, basic skills, and techniques. As the class progresses additional lectures can be used to present new material on more advanced skills. Follow-up procedures that include other teaching methods will be very beneficial after the initial lectures. Assessment cannot be made in a lecture, nor can feedback be provided to the student. The use of the lecture must be confined to the functions of motivating the students and informing them of expected accomplishments.

In order to achieve a degree of usefulness, lectures should be stimulating, well-prepared, and delivered in an enthusiastic and vivacious manner. For best results, the lecture should be supplemented by demonstration or experimentation. Since the lecture is such an important teaching method and is used in combination with other methods and techniques it will be discussed in greater detail later in the chapter.

Discussion Method

An immediate follow-up to the lecture is the discussion. Students become directly involved in this method, ask questions, and present their own ideas concerning the topic under discussion. This method usually works best with a small group because this allows each student the opportunity to express his ideas. Students are better able to develop ideas which will aid their skill acquisition through the discussion method. All students should feel that their contributions are welcome. Discussion may be used in skill activities immediately after students have performed the skill. Leading questions such as "How does it feel?" or "Where does the power come from?" may help students to think about the skill in exact terms. It is only when students think about skill that any definite decision-making process can occur.

The give-and-take of discussions offers the student a chance for verbal expression, quick thinking, and a place for examining his views. Several factors should be considered in the use of class discussion. The class size should be kept to twenty-five or less. This size not only permits the total class to become better acquainted and thus more spontaneous in expressing their views, but it also enables the teacher to keep the discussion on course. The teacher must have sufficient control of the class to prevent students from discussing each other rather than the problem under study. If the teacher notes any such tendency, he should remind the students that the study is problem-centered, not person-centered. At the same time, the teacher must carry the reins of authority lightly, lest the discussion become a student-teacher-student exchange. The teacher must keep tossing the conversational ball to the students, intervening only when necessary.

To assure the most effective results of class discussion, classes should be planned to include students from all levels of academic achievement and ability. The slow readers can become active participants by engaging in panel discussions or debates.

Group thinking and discussion constitute a cooperative enterprise. The contributions of each member must be meaningful or the discussion will become frustrating and a waste of time. The use of group discussion, leading to decision making, enables individuals within the group to accept new ideas, since these ideas may have group sanction behind them. Group discussions producing this effect should take precedence over personal likes and dislikes.

Lecture-Demonstration Method

Techniques used in the lecture method must also be used with the lecture-demonstration method. This method is also one of the leading methods used by physical educators and will be discussed in more detail later in the chapter. The demonstration may be performed by either the teacher, a student, or a group of students. It involves a visual experience which enhances the value of a verbal explanation and is quite impressive. This technique provides a unique experience for the students participating.

Verbal explanations are usually synchronized with a demonstration to provide a complete picture of the skill in question. Carefully chosen words can help a great deal in creating a mental image of what should be done and what it should feel like. In tennis, for example, some common phrases are "shake hands" for the forehand grip; "open and close the door" for the forehand swing; and "pull the arrow out of the quiver" for the serve. The ability, in most cases, can be developed and it has proven to be an invaluable aid to teaching. Each student should be able to formulate his own ideas as to how to move his body to duplicate what he has seen. The experienced performer should probably go through his performance several times showing different aspects that might possibly be troublesome to the beginner. Also, students should be allowed ample opportunity to ask pertinent questions about the performance.

Practice Method

Students are often able to help each other improve their motor skills. This process of interaction is very important in physical education classes. Homogeneous grouping permits the student to work with other students of similar skill and thus be able to offer constructive criticism and helpful techniques to each other. The teacher can closely observe those groups needing the most work and be less observant with those more advanced, knowing that those students are able to help each other.

After the student has grasped the basic concept of the skill there should be a period in which the student is allowed the opportunity to experiment with performance techniques. The initial attempts will probably be awkward but as additional attempts are made the student will begin to eliminate many of the early faults. Each additional attempt, with some help from the instructor and other students, should lead to a more accomplished performance. This method is incorporated in greater detail in Chapter 3, "Designs for Teaching."

Inquiry Method

The inquiry method is used to let students become involved in the teaching-learning process where they give input to solutions. A good teacher frequently poses questions that the students must think through and solve in order to keep abreast of the subject matter. One objective of the inquiry method is to develop the ability to do reflective thinking. Teachers may guide students in the inquiry method to discover solutions they never realized they knew. The inquiry method may be used in conjunction with projects, lectures, surveys, explorations, demonstrations, and laboratory experiments.

Project Method

The project method can be used in connection with a class enterprise or on an individual basis. Innumerable opportunities present themselves for using the project method.

The project method is employed during the class period with a small project that may be accomplished in a short period of time. The teacher should support the project method with related materials, discussion, demonstration, and related teaching techniques.

Oral Presentation Method

The oral presentation should be assigned to the individual student according to his interests and capabilities. The report should be well organized, concise, and accurate. The topics should be given well ahead of the time the unit is to be covered in class. The students should be instructed not to read their reports and to exclude trivia. They should know the material well enough to use only notes. An understanding by the class of the material in the unit being covered is the desired outcome of this method.

Part-Whole Method

One method by which physical skill is taught is the part-whole method. In this method, individual parts of the skill are learned before an attempt is made at performing the whole skill. This may be used in a variety of activities. In tennis, for example, footwork may be learned before the student ever holds a racquet and then these two steps are learned before the student attempts to hit a tennis ball. It is easily seen that this method is adaptable to many activities.

Whole-Part-Whole Method

Another teaching method used to a great extent is the whole-part-whole method. As its name implies, the students perform the skill at once, then go to basic instruction, and then perform the whole skill again. Some hold that this method is far more beneficial, because students may receive instruction in certain aspects of the skill that they know they need help with. An additional benefit of this method is that students who can already do the skill may move up to a higher level of difficulty at once without having to go through needless and time-consuming basic instruction. The whole-part-whole method is also another step in the direction of individualism.

Progressive-Part Method

In the sequential method, every skill is taught through a logical progression. This method is very often used with younger students. A prime example of this type of teaching method is the forehand stroke in tennis. By this method, beginning students first learn the basic footwork; next they may practice swinging an imaginary racquet by the mimetic technique; then they will begin hitting a tennis ball with their hand, still utilizing all of the stages they have learned before; then they will hit a tennis ball using a deck or paddle tennis racquet (or maybe just a short tennis racquet), and finally they progress to a regulation tennis racquet. (It must be remembered that this method has been simplified for purposes of illustration.)

FUNDAMENTAL PRINCIPLES

The teaching-learning process involves a complex array of factors which must be employed if effective teaching and learning are to take place. Before, during, and after teaching, the following principles should be kept in mind.

Teachers should be aware of factors affecting learning.

The learner is totally involved in any learning experience. Factors include: performance, physical qualities, human abilities, body type, height, weight, balancing ability, coordination, reaction time, movement time, the senses, perceptual mechanism, emotional state, level of skill, success, level of aspiration, sex and other genetic factors. The general physical and social environment should be suitable to the kind of learning taking place. The teacher should strive to increase pleasant emotions and decrease unpleasant emotions. It is necessary that the teacher understand students as a group, in addition to understanding them as individuals. Leadership is not a general trait; a good leader for a football team may or may not be a good leader for a discussion group, a research project, or an overnight hike. It is important that the teacher has objectives clearly in mind and organizes for learning in order to get results.

Teachers should have a knowledge of the principles that affect learning.

Good teaching is a matter of drawing out rather than of putting in. Good early instruction is necessary to prevent bad motor habits. Lasting education is not a matter of teaching-telling, but rather one of student-doing. The modern idea of a good teaching procedure most often implies the devising of learning experiences that drive directly toward the learning to be achieved. Effective learning is more likely to occur when a logical relationship exists between things taught. If learning is to be brought about there must be a problem, the learner must have a goal and purpose, and there must be a solution. Learning takes place better when students know where they are going, and that place is somewhere that they want to go.

Creating interest is an outstanding quality of good teaching. Learning must be directed toward something—a problem, content, etc. Begin where the learner is, relate the new to the old, adjust pace to learner's capacity. Things should be taught the way they are to be used. Learning must make sense to the learner, progress must be constantly appraised and redirected, and the purpose must be kept in sharp focus. Learning results through self-activity; it must engage a maximum number of senses. The most effective learning results when initial learning is immediately followed by application. Memorization alone is temporary unless put to use in a practical situation; activities that simulate use situations are most effective. Repetition, accompanied by constant effort toward improvement, makes for effective development of skill. Gross motor skills are usually *retained* longer than any other type of learning materials.

A teacher's attitude affects learning.

The teacher is a director of learning rather than a bearer of lessons. It is as important for the teacher to know the student as it is for him to know the subject matter. Kindness is the first quality of a good teacher. One of the biggest challenges to a teacher is the recognition of the true worth of each student. It is important to let the learner know that he is making progress; however, we must not mistake conformity for learning.

In the gymnasium, just as in the larger unit of American democracy, there can be no freedom without responsibility. The teacher should strive to develop leaders who can accept responsibility. A good teacher is a leader who develops other leaders.

Methods of teaching affect learning.

The aim of teaching is to help students achieve their objective. There is no single *method of instruction* appropriate for all teachers, for all students, or for all skills. In similar situations, different pupils may learn by the application of a variety of teaching procedures. Generally, there is no one best method. Teaching procedures should be developed for the accomplishment of specific learning objectives. They must fit the needs and maturities of particular students and the psychological relationships of the particular phases of the subject matter used. The right method for one teacher may be the wrong one for another. Learning may be facilitated by moving from the simple to the complex, from the known to the unknown, from the concrete to the abstract. The introduction of teaching *cues* and *aids* helps learning where traditional methods fail. Regardless of how long he has served the profession. no teacher should enter a classroom without a lesson plan developed for that specific class. The job of the teacher is to make a quick analysis of the learner, detect errors, explain the correction, and allow plenty of time for practice. Probably more important than correcting the error is to let the learner see the correct response to the whole act rather than just the individual parts alone. Frequent summaries and periodic reviews facilitate subject matter learning. Assignments which challenge the interests and abilities of the pupils stimulate improved study techniques.

Teachers should hold students accountable for learning.

The teacher cheats the student of part of his education unless he permits him to engage in all three of the closely related aspects of a learning situation; namely, planning the experience, carrying it out, and evaluating it. Students should be informed about what they are to look for in their tasks. This helps them organize their efforts to accomplish the task.

Learning must be challenging and satisfying. Motivation is essential if desired learning is to take place. Teachers should require standards suitable to the learner's ability and give appropriate and timely recognition to enhance learning. Ideal teaching procedures should provide for the development of initiative and self-direction. Students learn more when they are held to account for and are responsible for learning. Responsibility for the work involved in a learning situation should rest largely upon the pupil concerned after goals have been clarified and work processes defined. Evaluation is part of the teaching-learning process; get students into positions where they must constantly evaluate their own results. Examinations test the teacher as much as they test the student.

LECTURE AND LECTURE-DEMONSTRATION METHODS

The Lecture and Lecture-Demonstration methods are the most used of all teaching methods. Therefore, a more detailed description of these methods will be presented in this section.

Lecture Method

1. Introduction
   a. Develop student interest.
   b. Direct thinking toward desired objectives.
   c. Delineate scope of the lesson.
   d. Inform students of the value of the subject matter.
   e. Tell students what will be expected of them.
   f. Speak with enthusiasm.
   g. Talk to everyone including students in the back row.
   h. Be cheerful—face and talk to the class.
   i. Use showmanship and tell stories to create interest.

2. Presentation
   a. Speak loud enough to be heard without shouting.
   b. Keep the tone of voice friendly.
   c. Speak clearly and select words carefully.
   d. Make your points clear by using words that can be understood.
   e. Explain any unfamiliar or technical terminology.
   f. Use voice to give emphasis.
   g. Talk to everyone.
   h. Use correct pronunciation of words and avoid word repetition.
   i. Use teaching techniques when advisable (charts, blackboard, demonstration).
   j. Ask questions (try to get class interaction).
   k. Judge effectiveness, observe students' expressions.
   l. Use meaningful gestures but avoid habitual gestures.
   m. Use colorful yet accurate language.
   n. Use audio-visual techniques when appropriate.
   o. Go over main points more than once.
   p. Know your subject, be confident in yourself.
   q. Stimulate discussion.
   r. Employ humor in your lecture to add interest.
   s. Change the pace of speaking to make lecture more interesting.
   t. Keep interested in your topic.
   u. Use informal methods, yet hold respect of class.

3. Summary
   a. Recapitulate the main points of the material presented.
   b. Tie up any loose ends for the students.

c. Encourage discussion.

d. Organize material in the mind of the student.

e. Strengthen weak spots of instruction.

Lecture-Demonstration Method

1. Introduction
   a. Place students so they can all see and hear. Students should stand or kneel on one knee rather than sit, for better acquisition of kinesthetic cues.
   b. Introduce the activity taught using principles of lecture method (see Lecture Method).
   c. Relate skill to previous learning.
   d. Keep in mind the principles of teaching (see fundamental principles).
2. Demonstration
   a. Demonstrate the skill at operating speed.
   b. Use standard form and procedure.
   c. Use standard terminology.
3. Demonstration and Instruction
   a. Demonstrate skill again, giving a different view for the students.
   b. At each step of the procedure, state specifically what you are doing. Indicate teaching points.
   c. Give reasons why you are doing a particular skill a particular way.
   d. Explain fully any action that might not be observed if it were not pointed out.
   e. Remember, order of presentation is very important here. Know your activity and teaching progression.
   f. Point out relationship to previous learnings, e.g., badminton to basketball to tennis.
4. Repeat Demonstration and Key Points
   a. Repeat the activity at slightly slower than operating speed.
   b. Demonstrate so that students get a different view.
   c. Point out key points.
5. Summary
   a. Re-emphasize main points (repetition principle).
   b. Organize procedure in mind of students.
   c. Encourage discussion.
   d. Strengthen weak points of instruction.

3

DESIGNS FOR TEACHING

Suppose you have a ball you want to throw to someone. Don't throw it yet! What kind of a ball is it? A basketball? A football? A medicine ball? A baseball? Each kind of ball requires a different style or design for throwing. If it were a baseball one would normally use an overhand throw. If it were a basketball a two-hand chest pass might be used. Before throwing the ball, you had better look at your receiver. How far away is he? Is he watching you? Is he ready to catch the ball? Does he need a glove?

In this situation, the thrower is the teacher, the way the ball is thrown is the method, the specific grip, release, etc., that imparts spin to the ball are the techniques used, the receiver is the student, and the total process involved in the delivery of the ball to the student is the design. In teaching, as in this illustration, the design used will be selected on the basis of the subject matter and modified in terms of the student. The subject matter should not be presented until the student is ready to receive it, and, incidentally, if the throw goes wild the student can hardly be blamed.

A teaching design then is the overall plan or procedure a teacher uses to transmit subject matter to students. It may include one or more techniques and methods of teaching in the process.

The first design that is presented in this text is an introductory design which is particularly useful for prospective teachers in demonstrating the principles and techniques of skill teaching.

Prospective teachers, learning to teach, should select a simple skill, i.e., one which requires little movement on the part of the learner. Skills which provide beginning points for prospective teachers using this design include over-lapping grip in golf, Eastern forehand grip in tennis, waiting position in badminton, bunch-start "set position" in track, right-end offensive stance in football, left linebacker stance in football, basketball right forward defensive stance, etc.

INTRODUCTORY DESIGN

Phase I	**Introduction**
Phase II	**Teacher demonstrates and instructs**
Phase III	**Students tell, teacher does**
Phase IV	**Students tell and do**
Phase V	**Practice**

The Introductory Design is used in teaching a skill to a small group. This design may be used when a few students have failed to grasp the procedures for learning a skill when a large group design has been employed or this design may be useful in coaching situations where there is a small number of athletes to be taught and time for teaching the skill is not critical.

The Introductory Design is presented here because: (1) it illustrates the important steps necessary for learning a skill in greater detail than is possible with a large group; (2) it allows a teacher to demonstrate the ABCs of teaching a skill under controlled conditions (small number to grasp task), thus obtaining confidence in teaching ability; and (3) it allows a step-by-step procedure for the teacher to follow in teaching a simple skill to a small group. Good teachers are good technicians first, and this design aids in preparing teacher technicians. Before becoming a teacher one should first become a good technician, as is the case with almost any profession.

Phase I   Introduction

Purpose: Student warm-up.
1. Place students so all can see and hear. Students should stand rather than lean or sit for better acquisition of kinesthetic cues.
2. Introduce the activity to be taught—type of skill, why it is important to learn, mastery of the skill, etc.
3. Motivate. Be enthusiastic about the activity—enthusiasm is catching.

      a. Like what you are doing.

      b. Show an interest in students.

  4. Relate skill to previous learnings and to future learnings (carryover).

  5. Keep in mind the principles of skill-learning.

      a. Sequence: order of presentation is important.

      b. Early successes are beneficial to learning.

      c. Appeal to the senses in combination.

      d. Kinesthesia is important to learning.

      e. Repetition is a must in skill learning.

      f. Techniques, methods, and other principles must be considered.

Phase II   Teacher demonstrates and instructs

Purpose: To present the specific way the skill is to be performed.

  1. Demonstrate the skill at operating speed. Use standard form and procedure.

  2. Demonstrate skill again giving a different view for the students. At each step of the procedure, state specifically what you are doing (teaching points).

      a. Give reasons why you are doing the skill this way.

      b. Explain fully any action that might not be observed if it were not pointed out.

      c. Remember that order of presentation is very important during this phase of learning. It is confusing to the students if you have to say, "I forgot to tell you" or "I should have told you."

      d. Point out relationships to previous learnings—if students are familiar with any step or can transfer from previous learnings identify them for the student.

      e. Employ lecture-demonstration principles.

  3. Repeat the skill at slightly slower than operating speed (give students a different view). Indicate key teaching points.

      a. Order of presentation principle important.

      b. Repetition principle in operation.

Phase III   Students tell, teacher does

Purpose: To assure the teacher that students *know* what to do, how to do it, and the key points involved.

  1. Repeat the skill as each student in turn tells what to do, how to do it, and the key points involved.

      a. Remember, there are three things to learn about each step of the procedure: what to do, how to do it, and the physical movements involved.

   b. If the student is relieved of the responsibility for the physical action and the fear of doing something wrong, he can concentrate on procedure alone until it is right.

   c. To make a mental error in the classroom may seem trivial to a student, while making a physical error where the body is involved may be quite embarrassing. This step attempts to avoid this embarrassment.

2. After each student in turn has told what to do, how to do it, and the key points involved, you should ask good questions.

   a. The purpose of the questioning procedure is to make sure that the students really understand and are not just reciting what they heard in phase II.

   b. Make questions clear, brief, and challenging. Typical questions might be: "How do I do that?" "What do I do next?" "Why do we do it like this?" "Are my feet in the correct position?"

   c. Direct each question to the total class.

   d. Call on a specific student to answer. Insist on individual response.

   e. Evaluate answers in terms of understanding the points involved.

3. When you are assured that all students have a firm grasp of the procedure for performing the skill, move to phase IV.

Phase IV   Students tell and do

Purpose: To assure the teacher that the skill can be performed with the instruction given.

1. Each student in turn tells in advance of any movement what he is going to do, how he is going to do it, and then performs the skill.

   a. If a student forgets what to do or tries to do the wrong thing, stop him. Get him to review the procedure by asking questions.

   b. If student still does not recall the procedure, go back and take student through phases II and III again.

   c. Remember, the skill is new to the student, he is apt to be slow, faltering, and likely to make mistakes. Be patient.

   d. Don't take the activity away from the student. Students must do their own learning.

   e. Don't confuse the student with new instructions.

2. Insist on "correct" procedures. Remember that early successes are beneficial to learning.

   a. Point out those things a student does right rather than dwell on those things done wrong.

b. Praise rather than reprimand.

3. Let each student make all movements by himself.

4. When you are reasonably certain that students can perform the skill with some degree of success, move to phase V.

Phase V   **Practice**

Purpose: To improve performance.

1. Students perform the skill as you supervise and reinstruct when needed.
    a. Drill selected should be an individual drill, i.e., one in which you may observe each student individually to assure accuracy of movement.
    b. You should observe carefully for any deviation or variation in the steps of the procedure which may lead to faulty performance. If bad habits are observed, you should reteach that portion of the skill.
    c. Work for accuracy of movement and procedure first. Having familiarized the students with the procedure, begin to work for speed of movement.

2. Continue this phase as long as is needed to bring students to operating standard or as long as time permits.

INTRODUCTORY DESIGN

Phase I: INTRODUCTION

1. Sudents can see and hear
2. Students warm up
3. Procedure is related to previous knowledge
4. Teacher presents logical sequence
5. Teacher provides enthusiasm—motivation

Phase II: TEACHER DEMONSTRATES AND INSTRUCTS

1. Teacher indicates teaching points (one fundamental)
2. Teacher emphasizes teaching points
3. Teacher relates new procedure to previous learning
4. Teacher gives demonstration
5. Teacher uses logical order of presentation
6. Teacher repeats key points

Phase III: STUDENTS TELL, TEACHER DOES

1. Each student tells (what to do, how to do it)
2. Teacher asks good questions
    a. Formulates clear, brief, challenging questions

    b. Directs questions to class as a whole
    c. Calls on specific student
    d. Insists on individual response
3. Teacher evaluates answers and emphasizes correct response
4. Teacher is assured of students' knowledge of procedure

Phase IV: STUDENTS TELL AND DO

1. Each student does activity
2. Teacher stresses correct action
3. Teacher praises when warranted
4. If student forgets, teacher:
    a. Stops him
    b. Asks challenging questions

Phase V: PRACTICE

1. Teacher selects drill for individual help
2. Gives good drill instructions
3. Emphasizes accuracy of movement
4. Insists on procedure taught
5. Reteaches when necessary

CONSIDERATIONS

I. Management
1. Room conditions (heat, light, etc.)
2. Equipment and facilities availability
3. Class arrangement (sun, wind, crowding, etc.)
4. Placement of equipment
5. Use of equipment (minimum disturbance)

II. General Conduct of Lesson by Teacher
1. Uses voice effectively
    a. Speaks loudly enough
    b. Uses a friendly tone
    c. Demonstrates enthusiasm
    d. Speaks clearly
2. Talks to class
3. Makes eye contact
4. Judges effect (students' expressions, etc.)
5. Has neat appearance
6. Controls temper

7. Is cheerful
8. Has good posture
9. Develops student interest
10. Encourages student participation
11. Has thorough knowledge of subject

III. Distractions

1. Engages in negative teaching
2. Uses distracting mannerisms
3. Concentrates too heavily on discipline
4. Uses word repetition
5. Indulges in sarcasm
6. Uses habitual gestures
7. Is impatient
8. Adds instruction (phases III and IV)
9. Takes activity from student
10. Dwells on mistakes
11. Answers own questions
12. Allows loss of sequence
13. Creates class confusion

MILITARY DESIGN

Phase I	**Introduction**
Phase II	**Demonstration-instruction**
Phase III	**Imitation**
Phase IV	**Performance**
Phase V	**Individual drill**
Phase VI	**Team drill**
Phase VII	**Summary**

The Military Design is to be used in teaching physical education skills to large groups. This design has been used successfully by physical education teachers in teaching a variety of skills, e.g., a forehand in tennis, a dance step in social dance, physical fitness, routines to music, etc.

Phase I   **Introduction**

1. Place students in open military formation:

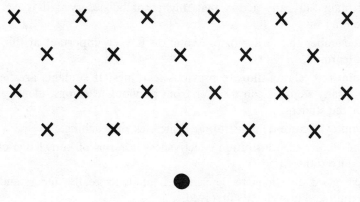

Figure 20
Open military formation

If equipment is needed, place equipment on the floor beside where students will stand in open military formation. If equipment is not used, have students count off by fours from roll-call formation and open ranks until in military open formation.

2. Make sure light, heating, and area are used to best advantage.
3. Introduce the activity to be taught (title of skill, why it is important, etc.). Use standard terminology. Define terms that students might not understand.
4. Motivate. Be enthusiastic about the activity—enthusiasm is catching. Relate stories of great performers of the activity, etc.
5. Relate skill to previous lessons.
6. Keep in mind the principles of skill-learning:
    a. Sequence of performance is important.
    b. Early successes mean a great deal to learning.
    c. Appeal to the senses in combination.
    d. Kinesthesia is important to learning.
    e. Repetition is a must.
    f. Use good techniques and methods.
    g. Let students do own job of learning.

Phase II   **Teacher demonstrates and instructs**

1. Demonstrate skill at standard speed. Use accepted form and procedure.

2. Demonstrate skill, giving students a different view.

    a. At each step of the procedure indicate the key points, what you are doing and why you are doing it.

    b. Explain fully any action that might not be observed if it were not pointed out.

    c. Remember that order of presentation is very important at this stage of learning.

    d. Point out relationships to previous learnings. If students are familiar with any steps or can transfer from previous learnings, identify them for the student.

    e. Employ lecture-demonstration principles of teaching.

3. Evaluate lecture-demonstration effectiveness in terms of knowledge of procedure transmitted.

    a. Ask good questions to determine if students really understand procedure and movements involved.

    b. Make questions clear, brief, and challenging.

    c. Direct each question to whole class but call on only one student to respond. Insist on individual student response.

    d. Evaluate answers. Praise when answers warrant.

4. When you are convinced students have an understanding of the movement involved, proceed to phase III.

Phase III   Imitation

1. Have students pick up equipment (if used) of the skill being taught.

2. Turn your back to class and assume waiting position to begin skill performance.

3. Perform skill very slowly, stopping at each step of the procedure to tell students what to do.

    a. As you perform one step, each student does the same step.

    b. Perform the next step, and the student when told to do so, imitates the same step.

    c. The student imitates the teacher at each step until the entire procedure is complete.

4. Students imitate teacher's performance.

5. Repeat your performance several times with students imitating movement each time.

    a. Talk students through each step by indicating key points.

    b. Make each repetition of the performance a little faster than the one preceding.

Example: Tennis forehand, ball landing close to body. *Teacher instructs.*

Step 1. *Take waiting position:* Body square to net, feet shoulder width apart, knees flexed, weight on balls of feet, head up watching ball, back straight, Eastern forehand grip hand waist high, racquet diagonally across body, other hand grasping throat of racquet.

Step 2. *Assume cocked position:* Drop right foot away from net perpendicular to sideline while pivoting on left foot, body perpendicular to net, eyes on ball, transfer weight to right foot while bringing racquet arm's length away from net, cock wrist, head of racquet up.

Step 3. *Swing:* etc.

Step 4. *Follow-through.*

---

6. Relate each step of the procedure to a number and repeat several times.
   a. Call out numbers at each step of the procedure while repeating performance.
   b. Increase tempo until speed and rhythm of movement is obtained. (1, 2, $\overline{3,4}$)
   c. Repeat several times until operating performance is obtained.
   d. Continue repeating performance until majority of students grasp performance.
   e. When the students are ready for it, students continue the activity by the numbers, without you to imitate (phase IV).

Phase IV   Performance

1. Assign one of the better performers in the class to call numbers in cadence of skill. (Have student calling cadence remain in formation.)
   a. Students no longer have an image to follow.
   b. Each student works to improve movement.
2. Move about class and observe movement.
   a. When incorrect movement is detected, stop that individual student (class continues to perform) and try to get student to recall procedure by asking good questions. If student does not recall procedure after prompting, reteach that phase of the skill.
3. Have student continue calling out numbers, increasing speed and in rhythm of skill until operating speed is approached.
4. Allow this phase of instruction to continue until some degree of uniformity is obtained.

Phase V   **Individual drill**

1. Select drill that allows you to observe each student individually.
2. Give clear instructions for drill, with minimum time spent for formation change and getting into drill.
3. Insist on procedure taught.
    a. Let students perform skill.
    b. Do not take skill away from students.
    c. Do not handle equipment.
    d. Stand in position to observe skill of each student.
    e. Have students perform skill on command.
    f. You should not be a part of the drill. Drill could continue even if you were not there. (You should concentrate on each individual's skill of performance.)
4. Emphasize accuracy of movement.
    a. Reteach that portion of the skill to students when necessary.
    b. Let students handle all equipment.
5. After each individual is observed and accuracy of procedure is assured for each student, rotate him into team drill. If possible, as students indicate to the teacher their mastery of the procedure, they should move to the team drill so that standing in line is kept to a minimum and participation approaches an optimum.
6. Continue individual drill or drills until all students have mastered skill procedure.

Phase VI   **Team drill**

1. Select a drill for optimum participation.
2. Make instructions clear, brief, and complete.
3. Teacher observes carefully for any deviation or variation in the steps of the procedure that leads to faulty performance. (If student can perform the activity with skill let him continue.) If bad habits are observed and performance is poor, the teacher should reteach that portion of the skill to the student.
4. After accuracy of movement is attained, work for speed of performance.
5. Have students handle all equipment.
6. Continue team drills, or combination drills, and lead-up games as long as needed to bring students to operating standard or as long as time permits.
7. For drills outside, be aware of sun, wind, water, holes in field, obstructions, etc.

Phase VII   **Summary**

1. Repeat demonstration-instruction.

2. Select student to perform skill and relate teaching points at each step of the way.

3. Ask good questions of class and call for individual student response. Evaluate answers.

4. Discuss activity taught.

5. Dismiss class.

MILITARY DESIGN

Phase I: INTRODUCTION

1. Equipment is placed in formation
2. Students line up by equipment
3. Facilities (lighting, heating, etc.) are adequate
4. Use of area is effective
5. Motivation is provided
6. New skills are related to previous knowledge

Phase II: DEMONSTRATION-INSTRUCTION

1. Teacher demonstrates at standard speed
2. Teacher demonstrates using different view
3. Teacher indicates key points
4. Teacher uses logical order of presentation
5. Teacher uses effective demonstration methods

Phase III: IMITATION

1. Students pick up equipment
2. Teacher (or skilled student) faces away from class
3. Teacher (or skilled student) performs, pointing out each step
4. Students imitate movement of teacher
5. Students repeat movement several times
6. Teacher relates each step to a number
7. Teacher calls numbers in skill rhythm
8. Teacher repeats exercise several times
9. Teacher continues performance until students grasp movement

Phase IV: PERFORMANCE

1. Teacher assigns student to call numbers
2. Teacher removes image
3. Student calls numbers in rhythm
4. Teacher observes each student
5. Teacher stops and reteaches incorrect performance
6. Teacher continues exercise until some degree of uniformity is achieved

Phase V: INDIVIDUAL DRILL
1. Teacher selects drill for individual help
2. Teacher gives instructions for drill
3. Teacher emphasizes accuracy of movement
4. Teacher insists on procedure taught
5. Teacher reteaches when necessary
6. Teacher is in position to teach individual student
7. Students handle all equipment

Phase VI: TEAM DRILL
1. Teacher selects drill for optimum participation
2. Teacher gives instructions
3. Teacher observes all students
4. Teacher makes optimum use of equipment and facilities
5. Teacher continues to teach where needed
6. Teacher emphasizes accuracy and speed of movement
7. Students handle all equipment

Phase VII: SUMMARY
1. Teacher gives demonstration
2. Teacher indicates teaching points
3. Students and teacher discuss

ATHLETIC DESIGN

Phase I	**Introduction**
Phase II	**Demonstration-instruction**
Phase III	**Repetition of performance**
Phase IV	**Student demonstration**
Phase V	**Individual drill**
Phase VI	**Team drill**
Phase VII	**Summary**

The Athletic Design for teaching has been found to be beneficial for teaching several activities, e.g., punting in football, the serve in volleyball, lay-up in basketball, backhand stroke in tennis, etc.

Phase I   **Introduction**

1. Place students so they can see and hear.

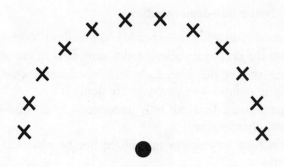

Figure 21
Instructional formation

 a. Use line markings on field or court when feasible so students don't crowd in and others can't see.

 b. A large semicircle is a good formation for instruction using this design.

 c. Students stand rather than lean or rest.

 d. Sun and wind may be a factor in teaching an outdoor activity—you should place wind to your back and sun to students' back during initial instruction.

2. Introduce the activity to be taught—name of skill, why it is important to learn, etc.

3. Motivate. Be enthusiastic—enthusiasm is catching.

 a. Show an interest in students.

 b. You are basic key to motivation—actions, psychology, exuberance, dedication, effort, organization, etc.

4. Relate to previous learnings and to future learnings (carryover).

5. Keep in mind principles of skill teaching.

 a. Be patient—students must do own job of learning.

 b. Use logical order of presentation.

 c. Appeal to senses in combination.

 d. Remember that kinesthesia is important to skill learning.

 e. Remember that each activity has own learning curve as well as individual learning curve.

 f. Make effective use of repetition, a must in skill learning.

 g. Use principles of teaching lecture-demonstration.

 h. Use good teaching techniques, methods.

i. Make use of equipment and facilities.

j. Get all students participating as soon as practical.

Phase II   Instruction-demonstration

1. Demonstrate skill at operating speed. Use standard form and procedures.
2. Demonstrate the skill again giving a different view to the students.

   a. At each step of the procedure, state specifically what you are doing (teaching points) and why you are doing it.

   b. If any terms used are not fully understood by all students they should be carefully explained.

   c. Explain fully any action that might not be observed if it were not pointed out.

   d. Point out relationships to previous learning.

   e. Employ lecture-demonstration principles of teaching.

   f. Use a logical principle of sequence—order of presentation is very important during this stage of learning.

Phase III   Repetition of performance

1. Repeat the skill again at slightly slower than operating speed. Give students another view. Stress key teaching points.

   a. Order of presentation principle important.

   b. Repetition principle in operation.
2. Evaluate lecture-demonstration effectiveness in terms of procedure.

   a. Ask good questions to determine if student really understands procedure and movements involved.

   b. Make questions clear, brief, and challenging.

   c. Direct questions to whole class so all students have an opportunity to formulate answer. Call on one student to respond.

   d. Evaluate answers—seek correct responses. Praise rather than reprimand.
3. When you feel students have an understanding of movements involved, proceed to phase IV.

Phase IV   Student demonstration

1. Select student to come to front of class to demonstrate and tell procedure for performing skill.

a. For obvious reasons the student selected should not be the best or the poorest in class.

b. The principal reasons for this phase of instruction are to:

   (1) Let students know that the activity can be performed with the instruction given.

   (2) Repeat instructions.

   (3) Point out areas where students might have difficulty in performing skill.

   (4) Indicate to the instructor if the instruction was or was not effective.

2. Instruct student to tell in advance any movement he is going to make, how he is going to do it, the key points involved, and then to perform the skill. (Get students to think about what they are doing.)

Example: Teaching Back Somersault on Trampoline

When you are in position to spot student ask him to repeat the key points before attempting the back somersault. Make sure student knows the key points involved and is thinking about them. Concentration is important. Student should say, "I will jump for control. After leaving the bed of the trampoline I will *EXPLODE,* that is, I will arch my back, throw my arms overhead, reach for the center of my back, throw head back, look for bed of trampoline and tuck (bring my knees against my chest). When my legs are overhead I will grab my shins. Next, I will open up, throw my hands up overhead, and I will land with my feet shoulder-width apart on the bed of the trampoline." When student knows what to do and has points well in mind let him perform skill as you spot.

---

3. After question and answer period to reinforce learning, move to phase V.

Phase V   Individual drill

1. Select drill that allows you to observe each student individually.

2. Give clear instructions for drill, with minimum time spent for formation change and getting into drill.

3. Insist on procedure taught.

   a. Let students perform skill.

   b. Do not take activity away from students.

   c. Do not handle equipment.

      d. Stand in position to observe skill of each student.

      e. Have students perform skill on command.

      f. You are not a part of the drill. Drill could continue even if you were not there. (You should concentrate on each individual's skill of performance.)

4. Emphasize accuracy of movement.

      a. Reteach that portion of skill to students when necessary.

      b. Let students handle all equipment.

5. After each individual is observed and accuracy of procedure is assured for each student, rotate into team drill. If possible, as students indicate their mastery of the procedure, they should move to the team drill so that standing in line is kept to a minimum and participation approaches a maximum.

6. Continue individual drill or drills until all students have mastered skill procedure.

Phase VI   Team drill

1. Select a drill for optimum participation.

2. Make instructions clear, brief, and complete.

3. Observe carefully for any deviation or variation in the steps of the procedure that leads to faulty performance. (If students can perform the activity with skill, let them continue.) If bad habits are observed and performance is poor you should reteach that portion of the skill to the students.

4. After accuracy of movement is attained, work for speed of performance.

5. Have students handle all equipment.

6. Continue team drills or combination drills and lead-up games as long as needed to bring students to operating standard or as long as time permits.

7. For drills outside be aware of sun, wind, water, holes in field, obstructions, etc.

Phase VII   Summary

1. Repeat demonstration-instruction.

2. Select student to perform skill and relate teaching points at each step of the way.

3. Ask good questions of class and call for individual student response. Evaluate answers.

4. Discuss activity taught.

5. Dismiss the class.

ATHLETIC DESIGN

Phase I: INTRODUCTION

1. Teacher makes sure students can see and hear
2. Teacher relates new activity to previous knowledge
3. Teacher uses logical sequence
4. Teacher provides enthusiasm—motivation

Phase II: DEMONSTRATION-INSTRUCTION

1. Teacher performs activity at operating speed
2. Teacher performs activity again, slowly, indicating key points
3. Teacher emphasizes teaching points (one fundamental)
4. Teacher relates new activity to previous lessons

Phase III: REPETITION OF PERFORMANCE

1. Teacher repeats performance at slightly slower than operating speed
2. Teacher shows class different view
3. Teacher restates procedure
4. Teacher gives demonstration (instruction effectiveness)
5. Teacher asks questions of class
6. Teacher repeats key points

Phase IV: STUDENT DEMONSTRATION

1. Teacher calls on student to demonstrate
2. Student demonstrates
3. Student points out key points
4. Teacher conducts question and answer period

Phase V: INDIVIDUAL DRILL

1. Teacher selects drill for individual help
2. Teacher gives instructions for drill
3. Teacher emphasizes accuracy of movement
4. Teacher insists on procedure taught
5. Teacher reteaches when necessary
6. Teacher is in position to teach individual student
7. Students handle all equipment

Phase VI: TEAM DRILL

1. Teacher selects drill for optimum participation
2. Teacher gives instructions
3. Teacher observes all students

4. Teacher makes optimum use of equipment and facilities
5. Teacher continues to teach where needed
6. Teacher emphasizes accuracy and speed of movement
7. Students handle all equipment
8. Teacher makes best use of available area

Phase VII: SUMMARY

1. Teacher demonstrates
2. Teacher emphasizes teaching points
3. Students and teacher discuss

BINARY DESIGN

Phase I	Introduction
Phase II	Instruction—demonstration
Phase III	Set A performs, Set B tells
Phase IV	Set B performs, Set A tells
Phase V	Individual drill
Phase VI	Team drill
Phase VII	Summary

The Binary Design is to be used in teaching simple physical education skills to large groups. This design has been used successfully by physical educators in teaching a variety of skills, e.g., self-defense, fencing, wrestling, tennis, tumbling, etc. This design frees the teacher to work individually with students to a greater degree than the previous designs.

Phase I   Introduction

1. Pair students according to size and ability and assign each pair to a station. If equipment is needed, place it on station for each pair, e.g., place foils, badminton racquets, etc., so that each pair has room to move freely without obstruction. If equipment is not used, students should be paired and given a position at a station or opposite one another.

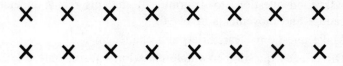

Figure 22
Paired formation

2. Make sure light, heat, and area are used to best advantage and that students are placed so that all can see and hear.

3. Introduce the activity to be taught (title of skill, why it is important, etc.). Use standard terminology. Define terms that students might not understand.

4. Motivate. Be enthusiastic about the activity—enthusiasm is catching. Relate stories of great performers of the activity, etc.

5. Relate skill to previous learnings.

6. Keep in mind the principles of skill learning.

    a. Sequence of performance is important.

    b. Early successes are important to learning.

    c. Appeal to the senses in combination.

    d. Kinesthesia is important to learning.

    e. Repetition is a must.

    f. Use good techniques and methods.

    g. Let students do own job of learning.

Phase II   Instruction-demonstration

1. Demonstrate skill at standard speed. Use accepted form and procedure.

2. Demonstrate skill, giving students a different view.

    a. At each step of the procedure point out the key points, what you are doing and why you are doing it.

    b. Explain fully any action that might not be observed if it were not pointed out.

    c. Remember that order of presentation is very important at this stage of learning.

    d. Point out relationships to previous learnings. If students are familiar with any steps or can transfer from previous learnings, identify them for the student.

    e. Employ lecture-demonstration principles of teaching.

3. Evaluate lecture-demonstration effectiveness in terms of knowledge of procedure transmitted.

    a. Ask good questions to determine if students really understood procedure and movements involved.

    b. Make questions clear, brief, and challenging.

    c. Direct each question to whole class but call on only one student to respond. Insist on individual student response.

    d. Evaluate answers. Praise when answers warrant.

4. When you are convinced students have an understanding of the movement involved, proceed to phase III.

Phase III   Set A performs, Set B tells

1. Give Set A the equipment, if needed, telling them to perform the task as Set B tells them what to do and how to do it.

2. Have Set B check Set A's performance of the steps of the procedure. Set B is relieved of the responsibility of doing the activity and can concentrate on the steps of the performance. Set A follows instructions given by Set B.

3. Tell Set A to be concerned with the physical performance and with getting the "feel" of the activity.

4. Observe both Set A and Set B, watching for deviations from proper performance. Place the responsibility for the execution of this phase on Set B; converse only with students in Set B, trying to get them to produce correct performance from Set A. The inquiry, questioning technique is used. By holding Set B *responsible* for this phase of learning, esteem and worth of the individual is developed in the learning process.

5. When you are reasonably certain that Set A has had sufficient time to run through the procedure, move to phase IV.

Phase IV   Set B performs, Set A tells

1. Have Set B exchange places with Set A as formed in phase III.

2. Give Set B the equipment, when needed, and tell them to perform the task as Set A tells them what to do and how to do it.

3. Have Set A check Set B's performance of the steps of the procedure, as Set B follows instructions given by Set A.

4. Again observe both Set A and Set B, this time placing the responsibility for phase IV on Set A.

5. When you are reasonably certain that Set B has had sufficient time to run through the procedure, move to phase V.

Phase V   Individual drill

1. Select a drill that allows you to observe each student individually.

2. Give clear instructions for the drill, with minimum time spent in formation change and getting into drill.

3. Insist on procedure taught.

   a. Let students perform skill.

   b. Do not take skill away from students.

   c. Do not handle equipment.

   d. Stand in position to observe skill of each student.

   e. Have students perform skill on command.

   f. You are not a part of the drill. Drill could continue even if you were not there. (You should concentrate on each individual's skill of performance.)

4. Emphasize accuracy of movement.

   a. Reteach that portion of skill to students when necessary.

   b. Let students handle all equipment.

5. After each individual is observed and accuracy of procedure is assured for each student, rotate into team drill. If possible, as students indicate their mastery of the procedure they should move to the team drill so that standing in line is kept to a minimum and participation approaches a maximum.

6. Continue in individual drill or drills until all students have mastered skill procedure.

Phase VI   Team drill

1. Select a drill for optimum participation.

2. Make instructions clear, brief, and complete.

3. Observe carefully for any deviation or variation in the steps of the procedure that leads to faulty performance. (If student can perform the activity with skill let him continue.) If bad habits are observed and performance is poor, reteach that portion of the skill.

4. After accuracy of movement is attained, work for speed of performance.

5. Have students handle all equipment.

6. Continue team drills, or combination drills, and lead-up games as long as needed to bring students to operating standard or as long as time permits.

7. For drills outside, be aware of sun, wind, water, holes in field, etc.

Phase VII   Summary

1. Repeat instruction-demonstration.

2. Select student to perform skill and relate teaching points at each step of the way.

3. Ask good questions of class and call for individual student response. Evaluate answers.
4. Discuss activity taught.
5. Dismiss the class.

BINARY DESIGN

Phase I: INTRODUCTION

1. Teacher makes sure of adequate facilities (lighting, heating, etc.)
2. Teacher pairs students
3. Teacher assigns each pair a station
4. Teacher assigns equipment to each pair
5. Teacher provides enthusiasm—motivation
6. Teacher makes sure that all can see and hear

Phase II: INSTRUCTION-DEMONSTRATION

1. Teacher demonstrates at standard speed
2. Teacher demonstrates—points out key points at each step
3. Teacher explains each step of procedure
4. Teacher repeats instruction
5. Teacher asks good questions
6. Teacher requires complete answers

Phase III: SET A PERFORMS, SET B TELLS

1. Teacher assigns Set A equipment
2. Set A performs skill
3. Set B observes
4. Set B checks performance
5. Set B reminds partner of step of procedure
6. Teacher observes each pair
7. Teacher reinstructs when necessary

Phase IV: SET B PERFORMS, SET A TELLS

1. Teacher assigns Set B equipment
2. Set B performs skill
3. Set A observes
4. Set A checks Set B's performance
5. Set A reminds Set B of steps of procedure
6. Teacher observes each pair
7. Teacher reinstructs when necessary

Phase V: INDIVIDUAL DRILL

1. Teacher selects drill for individual help
2. Teacher gives instructions for drill
3. Teacher emphasizes accuracy of movement
4. Teacher insists on procedure taught
5. Teacher reteaches when necessary
6. Teacher in position to teach individual student
7. Students handle all equipment

Phase VI: TEAM DRILL

1. Teacher selects drill for optimum participation
2. Teacher gives instructions
3. Teacher observes all students
4. Teacher makes optimum use of equipment and facilities
5. Teacher continues to teach where needed
6. Teacher emphasizes accuracy and speed of movement
7. Students handle all equipment

Phase VII: SUMMARY

1. Teacher gives demonstration
2. Teacher emphasizes teaching points
3. Students and teacher discuss

STATION DESIGN

Phase I	**Station organization**
Phase II	**Introduction**
Phase III	**Instruction-demonstration**
Phase IV	**Practice**
Phase V	**Summary**

The Station Design has been used by many physical education teachers and has been found an effective design in teaching skills of touch football, basketball, track and field, physical fitness, weight training, etc. This design is especially advantageous to the teacher as it frees him to work with individuals that need the most help.

Phase I   Station organization

1. Lay out stations around the gymnasium or field to make the best use of available space.

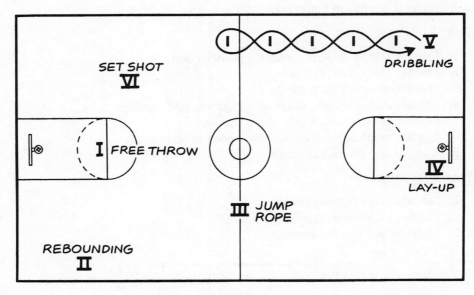

Figure 23
Station layout example

2. Number each station with a sign designation.

3. Post tasks to be performed at each station. If there are various levels of a task that lead to improved performance, outline them and place them at each station.

4. Make sure lights, heat, and area are used to the best advantage, stations are marked, and equipment in place.

Phase II   Introduction

1. Place students so they can see and hear.

2. Motivate. Be enthusiastic about the activity. Relate activity to previous learnings.

3. Introduce the activity to be taught (title of skill, why it is important). Use standard terminology. Define terms students might not understand.

4. Identify stations and tasks to be performed at each station for students.

Examples: Task levels

Variable	Level 1	Level 2	Level 3
Repetitions	5 punts 10 50-yd. dashes 15 free shots	10 punts 15 50-yd. dashes 20 free shots	15 punts 20 50-yd. dashes 25 free shots
Time	1-min. sit-ups 1-min. dribbling 5-min. jog	2-min. sit-ups 2-min. dribbling 10-min. jog	3 min. sit-ups 3 min. dribbling 15-min. jog
Quantity	1-sec. isometric chins 10-lb. curl 5-yd. out pass	2-sec. isometric chins 15-lb. curl 10-yd. out pass	3-sec. isometric chins 20-lb. curl Fly pattern
Quality	Knee push-ups One-hand set shot Dribbling right hand	Regular push-ups Dribbling one-hand shot Dribbling left hand	Spread-arm push-ups One-hand jump shot Dribbling alternate hands

Phase III   Instruction-demonstration

1. Take students to each station and give a demonstration and instruction of the task to be performed at that station.
2. Demonstrate the task at standard speed using accepted form and procedure.
3. Demonstrate skill again giving students a different view.
    a. At each step of the procedure point out the key points.
    b. Point out relationships to previous learnings.
    c. Employ lecture-demonstration principles of teaching.
4. Evaluate lecture-demonstration effectiveness in terms of knowledge of procedure transmitted.
    a. Ask good questions to determine if students really understand.
    b. Make questions clear, brief, and challenging.
    c. Direct each question to whole class and call on one student to respond.
    d. Evaluate answers.
5. When this phase of instruction-demonstration is completed at each station and you are convinced that students have an understanding of the tasks to be performed, proceed to phase IV.

Phase IV   Practice

1. Divide class into groups so that there will be about an equal number of students at each station.

2. Instruct the class in the rotation procedure for moving from one station to another to complete all tasks.

3. Instruct the class in the method for rotation, i.e., on whistle, when repetitions at a station are completed, etc.

4. Instruct class in the station level and how to move from one level to another during the unit.

5. Direct groups to stations.

6. Supervise performance and station rotation.

7. Work with students having difficulty.

Phase V   **Summary**

1. When all repetitions and sets for each station are completed, meet with class.

2. Review correct procedure at each station and demonstrate when needed.

3. Ask questions. Evaluate answers.

4. Point out objectives to be reached.

5. Conduct discussion.

6. Dismiss the class.

STATION DESIGN

Phase I: STATION ORGANIZATION

1. Teacher lays out stations
2. Teacher provides station designation
3. Teacher posts tasks
4. Teacher posts levels
5. Teacher makes best use of facilities and equipment

Phase II: INTRODUCTION

1. Teacher makes sure that students can see and hear
2. Teacher motivates
3. Teacher initiates activity warm-up
4. Teacher identifies stations and tasks

Phase III: INSTRUCTION-DEMONSTRATION

1. Teacher demonstrates at each station and instructs
2. Teacher demonstrates skill at standard speed
3. Teacher demonstrates again and instructs

4. Teacher evaluates effectiveness
5. Students perform at each station

Phase IV: PRACTICE

1. Teacher divides class
2. Teacher outlines rotation procedure
3. Teacher gives instruction on levels
4. Teacher assigns groups to stations
5. Teacher provides supervision
6. Teacher supervises rotation
7. Teacher gives individual help

Phase V: SUMMARY

1. Teacher meets class
2. Teacher reviews procedures
3. Teacher asks questions and evaluates answers
4. Teacher reviews objectives
5. Teacher leads discussion
6. Teacher dismisses class

TEAM DESIGN

Phase I	Introduction
Phase II	Instruction-demonstration
Phase III	Team assignment
Phase IV	Practice-supervision
Phase V	Summary

The Team Design may be used to teach any number of activities in physical education: touch football, basketball, gymnastics, speedball, soccer, etc. This design not only frees the teacher to work with individual students but frees the students to use their own initiative and aids in developing leadership.

Phase I   **Introduction**

1. Place students so they can see and hear.

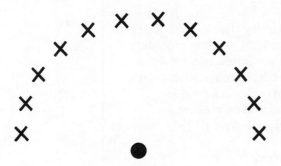

Figure 24
Instructional formation

   a. Use line markings on field or court when feasible so that students don't crowd in and others can't see.

   b. A large semicircle is a good formation for instruction using this design.

   c. Have students stand rather than lean or rest.

   d. Sun and wind may be a factor if teaching an outdoor activity—place wind to your back and sun to students' back during initial instruction.

2. Introduce the activity to be taught (name of skill, why it is important to learn, etc.)

3. Motivate. Be enthusiastic—enthusiasm is catching.

   a. Show an interest in students.

   b. You are basic key to motivation (actions, psychology, exuberance, dedication, effort, organization, etc.).

4. Relate skill to previous learnings and to future learnings (carryover).

5. Keep in mind principles of skill teaching.

Phase II   **Instruction-demonstration**

1. Demonstrate skill at operating speed. Use standard form and procedures.

2. Demonstrate the skill again giving a different view to the students.

   a. At each step of the procedure, state specifically what you are doing (teaching points, and why you are doing it).

   b. If any terms used are not fully understood by all students they should be carefully explained.

   c. Explain fully any action that might not be observed if it were not pointed out.

   d. Point out relationships to previous learning.

   e. Employ lecture-demonstration principles of teaching.

   f. Remember principle of sequence—order of presentation is very important during this stage of learning.

3. Give an instruction-demonstration of each skill to be practiced.

Example: Gymnastics—kip-up

Lecture demonstration of **arch-out on the trampoline**
                           kip-up on the mat
                           kip-up on the parallel bars
                           kip-up on horizontal bar
                           kip-up on the rings

---

4. Evaluate instruction given.

5. When students have a solid grasp of the procedure of the skills being taught, move to phase III.

Phase III   **Team assignment**

1. Divide class into teams. Appoint captains, select captains, or divide into equal groups and elect captains.

2. Assign each team to an area or piece of apparatus, etc.

3. If teams use different equipment, rotate to all equipment. If different equipment is not needed, as in touch football, for example, assign each team to an area.

Phase IV   **Practice-supervision**

1. Have teams led by team captains organize practice, with team captains giving leadership for improving team performance.

2. Supervise, answer questions, reteach when needed, and move from team to team.

3. Have teams continue to perform and to improve skills as long as you feel it is beneficial.

Phase V   **Summary**

1. Repeat instruction-demonstration.

2. Select student to perform skill and relate teaching points at each step of the way.

3. Ask good questions of class and call for individual student response. Evaluate answers.
4. Discuss activity taught.
5. Dismiss the class.

TEAM DESIGN

Phase I: INTRODUCTION

1. Teacher makes sure that students can all see and hear
2. Teacher introduces activity
3. Teacher motivates
4. Teacher relates new activity to previous learning

Phase II: INSTRUCTION-DEMONSTRATION

1. Teacher demonstrates at operating speed
2. Teacher demonstrates—teaches each skill
3. Teacher evaluates instruction

Phase III: TEAM ASSIGNMENT

1. Teacher assigns
2. Teacher sees that team captains are chosen
3. Teacher assigns teams to practice area

Phase IV: PRACTICE-SUPERVISION

1. Teams organize
2. Teacher supervises
3. Teacher helps when needed
4. Teacher circulates
5. Teacher evaluates performance

Phase V: SUMMARY

1. Teacher meets class
2. Teacher demonstrates skills
3. Teacher selects students to demonstrate
4. Teacher leads question-answer period
5. Teacher evaluates answers
6. Teacher initiates discussion
7. Teacher dismisses class

INDIVIDUAL DESIGN

Phase I	Individual schedule
Phase II	Introduction
Phase III	Instruction-demonstration
Phase IV	Practice-supervision
Phase V	Summary

The Individual Design is interesting to students since it satisfies individual needs and adapts subject matter to individual students. This design gives the teacher and students greater freedom in meeting objectives. It allows for individual differences in learning basketball, touch football, softball, soccer, physical fitness, etc. For example, students don't score equally well in all aspects of physical fitness; some students may lack arm strength and score well in other aspects while others may lack cardiovascular fitness, etc.

Individual programs may be planned to meet each student's needs. In a unit on basketball, some students may need an individual program stressing dribbling, while other students may need programs stressing other aspects of the game.

Most individual schedules in many activities may be anticipated and should be printed prior to the beginning of the unit. If programs and combinations of programs are developed prior to class more time may be given to teaching.

Phase I   Individual schedule

1. Anticipate individual needs.
2. Develop basic schedules for individual needs.

Example: Physical fitness

Individual schedules for developing:
Cardiovascular fitness
Strength
Flexibility
Abdominal endurance
Muscular endurance
Speed
Agility
Coordination

Example: Track and field

Individual schedules for:
Sprinters
Middle distance runners
Distance runners
Shot-putters
Broad jumpers
High jumpers

3. Prepare special individual schedules.

4. Print anticipated schedules.

Phase II   Introduction

1. Place students so they can see and hear.

2. Motivate. Show enthusiasm.

3. Introduce activity.

Phase III   Instruction-demonstration

1. Pass out individual schedules to all students.

2. Explain schedule tasks and objectives to be met.

3. Demonstrate tasks that students might not be familiar with.

4. Point out task techniques that might not be understood.

5. Conduct question-and-answer period; encourage class interaction.

6. Lead class discussion.

Phase IV   Practice-supervision

1. Have students proceed to perform tasks on individual schedules.

2. Supervise.
   a. Help when and where needed.
   b. Move throughout area.
   c. Be available to answer questions and explain tasks.

3. Have students continue individual schedule until complete or end of period.

Phase V   Summary

1. Conduct question and answer period.

2. Head discussion.
3. Encourage input from students on how to improve each individual schedule in order to better reach objectives.
4. Dismiss the class.

INDIVIDUAL DESIGN

Phase I: INDIVIDUAL SCHEDULE

1. Teacher anticipates needs
2. Teacher develops basic programs
3. Teacher prepares individual schedules
4. Teacher prints schedules

Phase II: INTRODUCTION

1. Teacher makes sure that students can see and hear
2. Teacher motivates
3. Teacher introduces activity

Phase III: INSTRUCTION-DEMONSTRATION

1. Teacher passes out schedules
2. Teacher reviews schedules
3. Teacher gives instruction-demonstration
4. Teacher provides for interaction
5. Teacher leads discussion

Phase IV: PRACTICE-SUPERVISION

1. Students practice
2. Teacher supervises

Phase V: SUMMARY

1. Teacher conducts question-and-answer period
2. Teacher leads discussion
3. Teacher encourages student input
4. Teacher dismisses the class

PROBLEM DESIGN

Phase I	**Introduction**
Phase II	**Presentation of problem**
Phase III	**Development of solution**
Phase IV	**Solution presentation**
Phase V	**Discussion and summary**

The Problem Design encourages originality and innovations and affords an opportunity for interaction of original mental and physical activity. The problem design is an effective means for creating new movements, developing new techniques, and solving game strategy.

Phase I   Introduction

1. Place students so all can see and hear.
2. Introduce activity (terms, skills, strategy).
3. Motivate class—enthusiasm, interest.
4. Inform class on problem design procedure.

Phase II   Presentation of problem

1. Describe the problem.

Example: Tumbling—forward roll

Find as many ways as you can to perform the forward roll.

Example: Basketball-tip

Your team has a 90 percent chance of getting control of the tip at the beginning of the game. How should you position each player on your team and what should be each player's movement at the tip to move for the score?

> Example: Track and field—high jump
>
> What is the best technique for you to use in clearing the bar in the high jump?

2. Answer questions.
3. When you are reasonably certain that class understands the problem, move to phase III.

Phase III   Development of solution

1. Have teams or individuals proceed to work stations to solve problems.
2. When progress seems stalemated, employ guided discovery or inquiry techniques.
3. When majority of class appears to have solutions to the problem, move to phase IV.

Phase IV   Solution presentation

1. Ask for individuals or teams, in turn, to describe and demonstrate their solution to the problem.
   a. Ask class to observe demonstrations.
   b. Evaluate, encourage, reinforce.
   c. Present good learning climate for timid students.
2. Critique each performance.
   a. Evaluate individual growth, not finished product.
   b. Be patient, praise when appropriate.

Phase V   Discussion and summary

1. Discuss solutions.
   a. Lead discussion.
   b. Encourage all to participate.
   c. Evaluate solutions with each student.
2. Summarize discussion.
   a. Enumerate possible problem solutions.
   b. Elicit other problems class might feel needs solutions.
3. Dismiss the class.

PROBLEM DESIGN

Phase I: INTRODUCTION

  1. Teacher makes sure that all can see and hear
  2. Teacher introduces activity
  3. Teacher motivates
  4. Teacher informs class of procedure

Phase II: PRESENTATION OF PROBLEM

  1. Teacher describes problem
  2. Teacher and students discuss problem
  3. Teacher answers questions

Phase III: DEVELOPMENT OF SOLUTION

  1. Students practice problem solving
  2. Teacher uses inquiry technique
  3. Teacher makes best use of area

Phase IV: SOLUTION PRESENTATION

  1. Teams or individuals describe solutions
  2. Teams or individuals demonstrate solutions
  3. Teacher critiques

Phase V: DISCUSSION AND SUMMARY

  1. Teacher leads discussion
  2. Teacher provides summary
  3. Teacher dismisses the class

INNOVATIVE DESIGNS

As you have probably suspected, there are an infinite number of teaching designs, only a few of which have been presented here. The teaching designs presented in this chapter have been found to be effective for teaching in physical education classes; however, there are other effective designs in existence and still others yet undiscovered that may be more effective. The use of mechanical learning aids such as the record player in teaching calisthenics to rhythm, or loop-film imitation in teaching basic gymnastic positions are examples of techniques and methods which may be used to develop designs not given in this chapter. Most of the teaching designs presented may be altered or combined in several ways to produce other designs.

As prospective teachers you should be thinking about how to better present subject matter to reach objectives. Recent literature indicates that innovative designs are being developed. All prospective teachers should become aware of new teaching designs that produce effective learning. The charge of the profession is for teachers to be cognizant of techniques, methods, and designs that are available to them in teaching and aware of those teaching designs that are effective for them.

You are the key to good teaching. You need to know what designs work for you. You should ever be interested in improving your teaching effectiveness. Don't be afraid to innovate or attempt to discover new ways of teaching.

4

ORGANIZATIONS
FOR LEARNING

Subject matter is organized to serve the function of convenience and economy in the use of the subject matter or to encourage learning. All types of formal organizations are artificial, that is, man-made. No organization of subject matter is natural in the sense that it merely grows in the accustomed organized form or in the sense that human beings just naturally think that way.

LOGICAL ORGANIZATIONS

Logical organizations are developed to serve the purposes of convenience and economy in the use of the subject matter classified. The essential element in all types of logical classifications of subject matter is the same kind or degree of likeness or similarity. Ease of learning may be determined in part by the structural relationship of the parts of the subject matter involved. Common examples of logical organizations used in physical education are classical organizations, sequence organizations, use organizations, competitive organizations, and project organizations.

Classical Organization

The *classical unit organization* organizes teaching from the simple to the complex. The first two periods of class are devoted to instruction in how the

```
1. Introduction
   a. Nature of the activity
   b. Movie of activity
2. Rules and regulations
3. Basic skills (simple to complex)
   a. Fundamental
   b. Combination
4. Lead-up games
5. Game competition
6. Testing
   a. Skill
   b. Knowledge
```

activity is played (scoring, rules and regulations, etc.) and showing the class a movie of the fundamentals and competition. On the field or court the class is taught fundamental skills, normally using the Military, Athletic, Binary, or Station teaching design. After three or four weeks in which the basic skills are learned, combination drills are used to integrate the basic skills learned, e.g., passing, dribbling, shooting in basketball. Lead-up games are played for two or three weeks, e.g., Newcomb in volleyball, 3-on-3 basketball, clock golf, etc. The remaining time in the unit is spent in playing the game followed by skill and written tests.

Sequence Organization

```
1. Introduction
   a. Nature of the activity
   b. Rules and regulations
2. Skills (taught in sequence game is played)
   a. Fundamental
   b. Combination
3. Lead-up games
4. Movie of skills and competition
5. Competition
6. Testing
   a. Skill
   b. Knowledge
```

The *sequence organization* is a logical unit organization which organizes skills for learning in the order that the game is played.

The first day of class, students are taught the nature of the game, rules and regulations, and basic skills involved. On the field or court for the next three to five weeks skills are taught in the order they are used in the game, e.g., in golf the woods are taught first, then the irons, and the putter last. Lead-up games such as clock golf are played as long as interest is high. During a rainy day when the class is forced inside, movies of skills and varsity-level competition of the game are shown. The rest of the unit is spent on game competition followed by skill and knowledge testing.

Use Organization

1. Introduction
   a. Nature of the activity
   b. Rules and regulations
2. Skills (those used most often are taught first)
   a. Fundamental
   b. Combination
3. Lead-up games
4. Movie of skills
5. Competition
6. Testing
   a. Skill
   b. Knowledge

The *use organization* for learning is a logical unit organization which classifies subject matter according to use, i.e., that which is used most is taught first and subject matter used least is taught last, etc.

Students are taught the nature of the game, then the rules and regulations, and then move to the field or court to learn the skills that are used most often in the game first; next often, next; etc. In golf, for example, the putter is taught first, followed by the irons and the woods. After the basic skills are learned, lead-up games are played to perfect and combine skills. A movie of the game is usually shown during inclement weather or when the gymnasium is needed by another group. The last part of the unit is given to game competition followed by skill and knowledge testing.

Competitive Organization *

The *competitive organization* for learning is basically a logical unit organization wherein the activity is learned through competition.

---

* The Competitive Organization is considered by some to be classified as a Readiness Organization.

1. Introduction
   a. Nature of the game
   b. Rules and regulations
   c. Movie of skills
2. Demonstration of skills and rules
3. Competition
   a. Ladder tournament
   b. Round-robin tournament
4. Individual instruction
5. Knowledge testing

Students are introduced to the activity at the beginning of the unit by instruction in the nature of the game, rules and regulations, safety precautions, etc., and a movie of skills is shown. Skills are demonstrated at the playing site and basic drills may be used to improve performance. The class is then divided into teams for participation in a round-robin tournament (e.g., basketball, volleyball) or assigned a position in a ladder tournament (e.g., tennis, handball). During competition or at designated intervals the teacher works to improve skills through individual and group instruction. At the end of the unit a written test is administered to the class.

Project Organization *

1. Introduction
   a. Project assignment
   b. Stated objectives
2. Project completion
   a. Activity performance
   b. Knowledge
3. Testing
   a. Performance
   b. Knowledge

Project organizations for learning are basically logical unit organizations in nature wherein students learn through completion of assigned projects.

Activities are introduced to students by stating objectives to be reached by the class in the unit and by assigning class projects for the unit: e.g., a unit in physical fitness might include ride a bicycle five miles ten times during the semester, swim one thousand meters twenty times during the semester, exercise

---

* The Project Organization is sometimes referred to as a Readiness Organization.

to videotape ten times, etc.; a unit in badminton might include read pp. 256–82 in the text, watch video, film and loop films on badminton, play thirty games of badminton during the semester, etc. Students are to fill out subproject performance/completion sheets each week. At the end of the unit the teacher administers a skill/performance test and knowledge test for the activity.

READINESS ORGANIZATIONS

Readiness organizations for learning are the arrangement of items or processes to be learned in an order that fits into the existing experiences or needs of the learners and serves to encourage learning. Some textbooks in educational psychology use the term psychological organization as a synonym for readiness organization.

Ease of learning (readiness) is determined by such factors as the relationship of the thing to be learned to the learner's experience, the relationship of the thing to be learned to a need or problem of the learner, and the satisfaction of the learner in increased control of new learning.

For most subject matter there is no established positive relationship between relative simplicity or complexity of structure and relative ease or difficulty of learning. For example, in a study with elementary school students it was found that it was easier (quicker) for students to learn to spell rocket, space, and Saturn than it was for them to learn to spell sat, rat, and cat. Even though the structure of the words in the first case was more difficult, the words had meaning to the learners and therefore they were ready to learn.

A good beginning point in teaching may be found at the point where subject matter crosses the experiences, needs, and interests of learners. This approach provides an introduction that challenges attention.

Common examples of readiness organizations employed in physical education are contract organizations, competency/performance organizations, game organizations, and pupil-participation organizations.

Contract Organization

Contract organization is a readiness unit organization that allows students to select contracts that meet their needs and give satisfaction to the learner through increased control of new learning.

Students are shown contracts for the unit or units from which they may select. Students are advised as to the number of points that must be earned for an A, B, C, etc., in each unit. Each contract is assigned a certain number of points which may be earned by each student. A worksheet is kept on each

1. Introduction
   a. Contract administration
   b. Required contracts
2. Contract agreement
3. Individual instruction
4. Contract fulfillment
5. Evaluation

student on which contract numbers, date completed, point value, penalty points, bonus points, and final scores are indicated.

Such contracts might include:

Bowling—25 points

Bowl ten games. Keep score sheet and return in packet. List the rules for keeping score and identify symbols used in scoring. You will be evaluated on accuracy.

Gymnastics—15 points

Observe a gymnastics meet at school, college, or on television. Make a list of the methods used in scoring gymnastic meets and identify stunts observed. Practice scoring routines and compare your score with judges at the meet. Keep a record of your score and the closest judge in each event and return in your packet.

Basketball—25 points

Take a written examination on basketball. You must score 85 percent or above to receive the contract points.

Each student sets his own pace but stipulates when he plans to complete the assignment selected. If a student fails to abide by the set schedule, penalty points are deducted. Bonus points are awarded by the instructor if the quality of the work merits.

Students may, if they desire, contract for a project that they would like to do, with the instructor assigning points if the project merits. The worksheet is kept up to date and grades are awarded on total number of points earned. No contract fails. If the work does not reach acceptable levels it is returned to the student and must be resubmitted.

Competency/Performance Organization

1. Introduction
   a. Lecture
   b. Demonstration
   c. Behavioral objectives
2. Pretest
3. Selected practice
4. Seminar
5. Posttest
6. Competency/performance evaluation
7. Conference redirection

The *competency/performance organization* for learning is a readiness organization that allows students to test out of that part of the module/program that proficiency has already been attained. Preplanning by the teacher sets up the competency/proficiencies that are expected in the unit with behavioral objectives written for the student.

Students are introduced to the unit by a lecture-demonstration of the various aspects of the unit with behavioral objectives outlined. If the learner feels that he knows enough about the unit, he may wish to show proficiency by taking a pretest. The test is scored immediately and a diagnostic profile prepared. If the learner is competent in some areas of the module/unit he will not have to study those areas already known. Those items missed by the learner will require that he work through that part of the module/unit containing missed items. If many items are missed, it will be necessary for the learner to work through the entire module/unit.

The instructor counsels with each learner in the areas where concentrated study is needed by that student. Once the learner reviews the terminal objectives, proficiency objectives, and learning tasks, he will develop an individual learning plan by choosing one or more routes to pursue from the instructional activities listed. The instructor will hold seminars or demonstration-teaching sessions that learners may attend if they wish.

Upon completion of the selected tasks the student will take a posttest over the material in the module/unit or, in some cases, take posttest performance tasks throughout the module/unit. Analysis of posttest results will determine competency/proficiency on the part of the student, and additional work needed will be determined in conference with the instructor. When the learner and the instructor are satisfied that competency/proficiency has been accomplished in a particular learning module/unit, the learner will progress to the next learning module/unit.

Game Organization

1. Introduction
2. Participation
   a. Lecture-demonstration
   b. Drill
3. Audio-visual presentation
4. Participation
5. Evaluation

Game organization is a readiness organization for learning that is a special attempt on the part of the teacher to adapt subject matter to the experience and interests of individual learners.

Students are introduced to the game with "play ball." As students see a need to learn the rules or develop skills they seek out the expertise of the teacher. In tennis for example, the first day the class meets it divides up and plays tennis. If there is a conflict or a need to learn whether a tennis ball hitting on the line is good or not, the teacher is available to answer questions. When students see a need to develop a better backhand in tennis, the teacher takes them aside and teaches the skill and implements the teaching with drill (any design in chapter 3 may be used). As soon as skill is developed to suit the needs of the learner he goes back to playing the game.

Students are helped by the teacher when asked to do so. The teacher is always available to answer questions, to teach skills, etc. As soon as a particular learning has been accomplished to the satisfaction of the learner he returns to playing the game.

Sometime during the semester, on a rainy day or otherwise, the class is shown audio-visual materials of players, rules, skills, etc. Now that students have become acquainted with the game, the explanation of the rules, expert skill, etc., on the film has more meaning and significance for the learner. For example, after watching a good tennis player on film use the American twist serve, students may be motivated to emulate him and seek the teacher's help in developing this skill. As soon as skill is developed in a particular area, the learner returns to playing the game.

The method of evaluation chosen depends on the objectives set for the unit. Some behavioral objectives besides skill and knowledge, which are sought with this organization for learning, are development of the play spirit, self-initiative, sociability, and fun.

Pupil-Participation Organization

1. Inquiry
2. Classification of needs
3. Index of interests
4. Selection of units
5. Selection of means to reach needs and interests
6. Participation
7. Pupil-teacher evaluation

Pupil-participation organization for learning is a readiness organization that fashions learning to the learner's experiences, needs, and interests and gives the learner satisfaction by increasing control over the new learning.

The instructor begins the unit using the inquiry method to determine student needs, interests, and aspirations in the course. Needs are classified and interests cataloged, with students selecting activities needed to reach their objectives. Options available for reaching determined needs and interests are discussed with students finally determining their own option or route to follow.

When selection of the options to follow are made, students develop along option guidelines at their own rate of achievement. Options may be selected as a group, or subgroups may select different objectives. For example, one subgroup of the class may want to learn more about movement exploration whereas another may want to know more about control of body weight; still another may want to develop cardiovascular fitness and others may want to have fun and play games.

Needs and interests of the class are usually given priorities and programmed by the class to meet these needs. Students and teacher are involved in the planning, as well as in the means of reaching desired objectives. The path that the organization for learning takes depends on the experiences, needs, interests, and learners' insights into the means for developing these areas.

As the planning and organization for each unit is pupil-oriented, so is the evaluation. Through conferences, teacher and learner evaluate the extent objectives are reached during the unit. This organization is pupil-centered and allows for student freedom in determining his own destiny in learning in physical education.

5

RESEARCH IMPLICATIONS

Every profession must follow its research findings if it is to stay abreast of the times. Physical education has yet to become a science since many of the conditions needed to produce effective teaching are not known. Many implications however, may be deduced from the research presented in this chapter. The implications are left to the reader since there is not enough evidence to establish them as principles. It is hoped that as each person reads this chapter he will deduce implications suggested by the research and become interested in adding to research in the area of teaching strategies.

It is rather difficult to divide present research into the areas of teaching techniques, methods of teaching, teaching designs, and organizations for learning since scholars in our field, in the past, have not used standard terminology. For example, in one study the whole method will actually be a method of teaching as defined in this book, but in another instance an author may be referring to an organization for learning. As you read the evidence presented in this chapter feel proud that the area of study, strategies for teaching physical education, is attempting to become a science.

IMPLICATIONS FOR TEACHING TECHNIQUES

This section is divided into three divisions, general techniques, mechanical techniques, and audio-visual techniques. While research in these three areas is extensive, when one focuses in on any one technique the evidence is very scant.

There are, however, several general implications that the reader may draw from the studies presented.

General Techniques

Davies (1945) conducted a study to determine the effects which tuition during practice had on the process of learning the complex motor skill of archery. It was concluded that the tuition group started at a higher level of performance than an uninstructed group, as they were given instruction prior to the first test. The tuition group progressed at a faster rate than did the nontuition group during the beginning and later stages of learning.

Dowell (1973) found no difference between a competitive and a cooperative learning environment on athletes or nonathletes in learning a novel game strategy.

Battig (1956), investigating the transfer of verbal pretraining to motor performance, found that the amount of transfer that occurs from verbal pretraining depends on the complexity of the task.

Deese and Kaufman (1957) examined the effects of sequential structure upon recall of verbal material. They pointed out the complexities involved in organizing the presentation of stimuli in order to achieve optimum results.

Malina (1969) in a study of the effects of varied feedback information on throwing speed and accuracy, found that feedback was important to the success of throwing. In a study of feedback as a motivator in swimming, Rushall and Pettinger (1969) found that feedback was important to the success of students in swimming. In a study to determine the effect of feedback in the learning of golf skills, Thompson (1969) found feedback improved the success of students in the performance of golf skills.

Brightwell (1969) found that there is no significant difference in the achievement of tennis skills among men and women when taught in coeducational or segregated situations. This suggests that perhaps there is no reason to separate men and women in some activity classes.

Woods (1967), in a study of the effect of varied instructional emphasis upon the development of a motor skill, found that the most desirable results were obtained by equal and simultaneous emphasis on both the velocity and accuracy variables.

Comrey (1953) investigated the relationship of the performance of the group to the abilities of the performers that made up the group. His groups were actually pairs. He concluded that group performance is dependent on the average of the scores of the individuals on a similar task.

William Johnston (1966) found that when performing complex motor tasks communication between members of the team has a disruptive effect on transfer and that training in skills that are specific to the task benefits transfer.

Mohr and Barrett (1962) found that an understanding and application of mechanical principles effects greater improvement than instruction without reference to these principles. Knowledge of these principles may be gained by viewing the performances of expert performers. Application of principles may be visualized by allowing the student to view and analyze his own performance on film.

In an experiment to test the effectiveness of learning from a programmed text as compared with a conventional text that covers the same material, Daniel and Murdoch (1968) found that students using the programmed text scored higher on a comprehensive test. In comparing the effects of self-instructive material in learning selected motor skills and no instruction, Jarvis (1967) found a significant improvement in children using self-instructive materials over the control group that did not use the material.

In teaching large groups in archery and badminton, Kingsley (1971) compared the spaced-unit method and the continuous-unit method and found no significant difference in final skill level. Webb (1961) explored the effects of varying amounts of implicit rehearsal and the effects of the spacing of these rehearsals on the amount of learning that could be demonstrated in archery skills when implicit rehearsal was combined with overt practice. No significant effects were found.

In a study of the effectiveness of visual cues and kinesthetic cues in the teaching of the overhand throw to seventh-grade girls, Wyatt (1969) found that a visual cue (viewing a loop film of a woman performing the overhand throw) was a more effective learning aid than the kinesthetic cues (use of a weighted badminton racquet in the overhand throwing pattern and the use of a jump rope in the same pattern to achieve a snapping action), particularly for poorer throwers.

Battig (1954) attempted to determine the role of visual cues, kinesthetic cues, and verbal cues in the acquisition of a precise level-positioning movement. He concluded that standard practice was superior, followed by verbal stimulus, kinesthetic response, verbal response, and verbal stimulus-kinesthetic response. It was concluded that training on any modification of the standard task may even produce negative transfer.

Hornak (1972) found that by giving speed emphasis, accuracy emphasis, and simultaneous emphasis on both components in the teaching method, or by giving simultaneous emphasis on speed and accuracy throughout the learning period, produced superior results in teaching the straight instep kick in soccer than by giving accuracy emphasis, speed emphasis, and simultaneous emphasis. Reilly (1971) tried to determine which instructional method (speed, accuracy, or speed and accuracy) should be used during the initial stages of skill acquisition in fencing. Results showed no significant difference in performance among the three groups.

Minaert (1950) in a study to determine the value of dry skiing in learning three maneuvers, found that in all three maneuvers the group that had dry-ski instruction was significantly better than the group that did not have dry-ski instruction.

Grebner (1969) found that teaching different methods of drawing the bow in archery had no effect on the success of the class in achieving desired results. He implied that methods of performance are individual rather than group and that these individual differences must be considered.

Godlasky (1955) found no difference in the effectiveness of teaching the crawl stroke to beginning swimmers for speed and distance with and without teaching the dog paddle initially.

Mechanical Techniques

Brown (1970) found that by using a suspended shuttle device with a release mechanism in addition to regular instruction was beneficial in learning selected badminton skills for college women. The device was particularly beneficial in developing the clear and smash strokes. In addition, Brown concluded that women who had had softball or tennis experience appeared more proficient in their ability to learn overhead strokes in badminton.

Henschen (1972) found that boys and girls practicing at a small basket improved their shooting accuracy in basketball significantly more than when practicing at a regulation basket.

Matthews and McDaniel (1962) found that the use of the Golf-Lite was beneficial to most of the students who used it, as an aid to help them hit a target one hundred and fifty yards away with a five iron.

Kaye (1965) conducted an experiment to determine the effect of using a waist-type flotation device as an adjunct in teaching beginning swimming skills. He found that the students using the flotation device during training were able to swim farther than those who had not used the flotation device during training.

Solley and Borders (1965) investigated the effect of the Ballboy, a device that projects tennis balls at regular intervals and at a fixed trajectory, on teaching a fundamental tennis stroke to beginners. They found that this device is very useful in achieving skills. They also found that traditional teaching methods should be reinforced with mechanical aids even though they may hamper transfer.

Takacs (1966) found that shooting free throws at a small insert basket produced significantly greater accuracy than no practice but did not produce a significant difference from shooting at a regulation basket even though there was an 8 percent free throw shooting accuracy advantage by the small basket group.

Lindeburg and Hewitt (1965) attempted to discover the effect of an oversized basketball on shooting ability and ball handling. They found that the larger ball had no effect on shooting ability or on the dribble test. It did have an effect on the ability to pass the ball against the wall. They concluded that the oversized ball used in the experiment was not large enough to have an appreciable effect. Layton (1972) found that a basketball training glove did not increase shooting accuracy.

Nelson, Dailey, and Wessel (1963) investigated the use of the Alley-Spotting Target in the development of accuracy in spot bowling with beginning bowling classes and concluded that it failed to bring about improved performance. Nyce (1972) found no advantage in using a lightweight bowling ball as a supplement teaching aid in teaching beginning bowling. To study the effect of limited visibility in teaching women bowlers spot bowling, Gansel (1971) used goggles to aid the women. She found that with women bowlers the use of goggles did not improve bowling ability as measured in her study.

Nichols (1972) investigated distance, velocity, and angle of release of a thrown ball utilizing a variety of ball-throwing activities including a device aimed at patterning the angle of release. No significant differences between treatment groups were observed over the twelve-week period.

McCatty (1966) studied egg-shaped polystyrene foam plastic products in an experiment. He concluded that they did not help the nonswimmer learn the skills in swimming any sooner.

MacFarlane (1971) compared two methods of teaching the forehand tennis stroke to nine- and ten-year-olds. She found that there was no difference between teaching nine- and ten-year-olds the forehand stroke by either using the regular tennis racquet or using the sequential method of learning by first using a paddle.

Audio-Visual Techniques

Karlin and Mortimer (1962) investigated the effects of visual and verbal cues on learning a motor skill. They found that verbal and visual cues affect learning and retention. They also pointed out that the presentation of these cues must be timed so that they are presented at the right moment, when the student is ready for them.

Megale (1972) undertook a study to determine the effectiveness of rhythmic accompaniment as a teaching supplement to the conventional method of instruction in the development of selected sport skills. He reported that the addition of rhythmic accompaniment to the conventional method of instruction was superior to the conventional method without rhythmic accompaniment.

Lockhart (1944) found that the use of motion pictures as analytic aids was a valuable supplement to the regular instructional program. Watkins (1963) reports that batters who view films of their own performances can significantly decrease the number of faults in their batting style as opposed to batters who do not view motion pictures of their batting.

Londeree (1967) made a comparison in the use of motion pictures and flash cards in football play recognition. He concluded that motion pictures provided quicker recognition of formations by the defense, while flash cards seemed to work better for the recognition of defenses by the offense.

Hawthorne (1961) studied the effects of the 8-mm slow-motion picture as a device for improving golf form. She concluded that the 8-mm slow-motion pictures were an effective aid in improving golf form. Fowler (1955) investigated the value of the slow-motion picture as an aid in the teaching of tennis skills. She found that the group viewing slow-motion pictures showed a higher mean gain than did the group which received regular instruction. In a study designed to determine the effectiveness of slow-motion films on performance in the high jump, Priebe and Burton (1939) found that analysis of the student performance using slow-motion films made for faster progress and better achievement. Also, to a large extent, the initial period of trial and error when switching styles of high jumping is eliminated. They also found that using illustrations of good form in slow-motion pictures was superior to verbal and physical demonstrations in improving performances.

Drowatzky (1971) found that video feedback improved learning of a balance skill performed by college women. Morgan (1971) compared verbal and visual cues in teaching beginning swimming to college women. The videotape feedback group improved significantly in tests of speed and power and both the verbal and videotape groups were significantly better than a control group in a test of power; however, the control group also improved significantly on the speed test. In determining the effect of television replay as a technique in teaching beginning swimming skills, Green (1971) found that with both beginning and advanced swimming students videotape replays were significantly better than the traditional method in improving performance.

Moore (1971) found cartoon illustrations to be ineffective in the attainment of tennis knowledge although it was found that the use of audio-visual aids was helpful to the teachers in their class preparation and in supplementing instruction.

Gray and Brumbach (1967) conducted a study to determine the effect of the daylight projection of film loops, using the Technicolor Instant Motion Picture Projector and the Magi-Cartridges, on the badminton playing ability of male college students. Except for the film loops, the experimental and control group were instructed in the traditional manner. They concluded that the audio-visual equipment were practical aids for teaching sports skills and that the loop films appeared to hasten the learning of badminton for beginning male students, but that the early advantage of viewing the films was not maintained.

Nelson (1958) studied the effect of slow-motion loop films on the learning of golf. One group learned golf with the aid of explanation-demonstration and slow-motion loop films while the other group learned beginning golf with the aid of explanation-demonstration. He found that slow-motion loop films improved the learning of golf in the later stages of learning, but not in the early stages. He found no significant difference between groups.

Dresser (1961) studied junior high school students to determine the value of loop film as a supplementary aid in teaching the crawl stroke in swimming. The teacher demonstration method was used to teach both groups, with the experimental group receiving loop film as a source of reference, self-help, and correction of errors. It was found that supplementary loop film did not influence the learning of the crawl stroke.

Camp (1969) conducted a study to determine the effects of viewing loop films on tennis skill and form while hitting a forehand drive and backhand drive. It was concluded that the addition of loop film to the traditional teacher-demonstration verbal-explanation method of teaching does not appear to facilitate the learning of tennis skills more than the traditional method itself, nor does it enhance the improvement of tennis form.

Anderson (1970) found no significant effect in the use of filmed model performances with three kinds of feedback on learning the short golf swing. Spencer (1961) found no difference in the use of movies, slides, or demonstrations as visual aids for teaching movement patterns in beginning modern dance.

Brown and Messersmith (1948) compared the relative progress of tumbling classes taught with and without the use of motion pictures. It was indicated that there was no difference between the groups taught with the use of motion pictures and those taught without the use of motion pictures.

Hixson (1970) concluded that, at the very least, instruction that used television is no worse than instruction that does not use it. Del Rey found that videotape feedback improved form and accuracy during acquisition of a motor skill, in a structured environment; however there was a significant improvement in latency in the unstructured environment. Rhea (1970), in a study at Wake Forest University, concluded that the use of a videotape replay, when substituted for a part of actual class practice time, was as effective as traditional process of continuous instruction. Harless (1970) concluded that conventional instruction and videotape recordings used in conjunction with conventional instruction were equal in their ability to assist in improving performance in beginning badminton, golf, and tennis, regardless of the stage of instruction at which they were used.

In a study of videotape instant replay as a teaching technique in beginning bowling classes Carmichael (1970) studied sixty male college students in two beginning bowling classes. One group was taught by the traditional method while the other had the advantage of self-analysis through the videotape recorder during the ten-week period of the study. He found no difference in bowling skill between the two classes.

Meyer (1969) reported no significant differences after supplementing bowling instruction with videotape in college bowling classes, but concluded that it enabled the instructor to make more accurate evaluation of bowling form.

Conry (1969) studied the effectiveness of the use of video tapes in learning beginning fencing. An experimental and control group received identical instruction except the experimental group was supplemented with the use of video tapes. The investigator concluded that observation of skilled performance and of own performance on videotape did not seem to result in greater skill development or increased knowledge, but that the physical practice time needed was less.

Lundquist (1969) studied the immediate knowledge of results via videotape replay and its effect on the learning of selected football skills and found no significant differences resulted from supplementing football skills instruction with videotape replay.

In a study to determine the effectiveness of using the videotape recorder in teaching gymnastic skills, Huffty (1970) reported no significant difference between the experimental group using the videotape recorder and the control group not using the videotape recorder.

Penman, Baurtz, and Davis (1968) studied the effects of teaching sports skills with and without an instant replay videotape recorder. Their investigation of teaching beginning trampoline with videotape indicated that there was no significant benefit in using the instant replay. Penman (1969) studied the relative effectiveness of teaching beginning tumbling with and without an instant videotape recorder. He found no differences between the group with traditional instruction and that group supplemented with videotape. In a study of the effect of the use of the videotape recorder as an aid in teaching the volleyball serve, Reid (1971) found no difference in using the videotape recorder.

IMPLICATIONS FOR PRACTICE

Egstrom (1964) studied six groups of college students who were right dominant to determine the effects of varying emphasis on conceptualizing and manual practice during the early learning of a novel ballistic gross motor skill. The data collected indicated that the five conceptualizing and manual practice methods were more effective in changing performance than was practice limited to taking three tests. It was also found that alternating periods of emphasis on conceptualizing and manual practice was as effective as successive periods emphasizing manual practice. Dunham (1968) concluded that teachers of motor tasks should direct practice patterns toward the strengthening of specific weaknesses without regard for practice ordering.

Beckow (1944) investigated the effects of a schedule of loop-film-aided mental practice upon learning the badminton short and long serve. He concluded that mental practice through the use of loop films can improve performance of a gross motor skill and that it appears to be more effective in improving performance of skills which require more precision and fine control than skills which are explosive or dynamic in nature.

In a study of mental practice, physical practice, and a combination of mental and physical practice in learning the long serve in badminton, Mitchell (1956) found that the mental practice group and the combination of mental and physical practice group improved more than the physical practice group in learning the skill.

In a study of the underhand basketball free throw Huffman (1954) compared a mental practice group, a physical practice group, and a control group. It was concluded that skill in performing the underhand free throw was significantly improved using mental practice but that mental and physical practice were equally effective in improving the underhand free throw.

Jones (1965) compared the learning of the hock swing upstart in gymnastics under different conditions of mental practice without support of demonstration procedures or physical practice. It was concluded that male university students could learn a gymnastic skill by reading a mechanical analysis and mentally practicing the skill. It was also concluded that undirected mental practice was superior to directed mental practice.

Waterland (1956) found in combining mental practice with kinesthetic perception that mental practice aided in learning bowling skills when the practice preceded overt physical performance. Shick (1970) conducted studies to determine the effects of mental practice on improvement in serving and volleying skills in volleyball. The mental practice group scored significantly better on the serve test than did the no practice group, and three minutes of mental practice yielded better results in comparison to one minute.

Hammer and Natale (1964) compared a group that learned touch typewriting without motor involvement with a group that learned through the traditional method with motor involvement. It was found that touch typewriting could be taught successfully without the use of typewriters and that greater initial accuracy was developed when learning took place without motor involvement.

Halverson (1949) compared the effectiveness of a mental practice method, a demonstration method, and a kinesiological method of teaching the basketball one-hand push shot. He concluded that all three methods were effective in developing skill in the one-hand push shot, that mental practice was not as effective as actual practice and that there was no significant difference between the effectiveness of the kinesiological and demonstration methods.

Weeks (1970) found that traditional classes were significantly better than conceptualization-practice technique classes in average velocity, velocity points, and average distance in golf.

Corbin (1967) concluded from his results that physical practice was the superior type of practice for learning motor skills, and that mental practice facilitates actual skill performance after controlled physical practice. Mental practice seemed to be better utilized when based on experience and when actual practice preceded performance of the skill.

Kelsey (1961) studied the effects of mental and physical practice on muscular endurance and found that both mental and physical practice produce significant gains in muscular endurance, but that physical practice was more effective than mental practice in increasing muscular endurance.

In comparing the effects of physical and mental practice Stebbins (1968) found that in learning to throw rubber balls at a target, mental practice alone did not produce improvement and that the greatest amount of improvement occurred by using a combination of practice conditions.

Burns (1962) determined the effect of physical practice, mental practice, and mental-physical practice on the development of the skill of dart throwing. It was concluded from this study that the groups which followed a physical practice schedule or a combination mental-physical practice schedule improved significantly, while the group participating in mental practice alone did not show a significant gain.

Clark (1960) compared the effect of mental practice with that of physical practice in the development of the Pacific Coast one-hand foul shot. Both the physical and mental practice groups showed significant gains with the mental practice group almost as effective as the physical practice for the varsity and junior varsity groups, but not as effective for the novice group.

Tufts (1963) concluded that mental and physical practice were equally effective in maintaining both bowling performance and accuracy for intermediate bowlers but that neither group showed significant improvement in bowling performance or accuracy.

Wills (1965) found, in teaching boys to throw a football for accuracy, that mental practice and physical practice both improved significantly but that there was no significant difference between the two groups.

Chui (1965) found that the Golf-O-Tron, an electronic device that simulates golf by using a modified computer coupled with colored photos of a selected golf course, did not significantly affect improvement in golf skill over the conventional practice range method.

Corbin (1967) compared the effects of mental practice and combined mental-physical practice as compared to physical practice in the development of the skill of wand juggling. He concluded that mental practice alone was not effective in developing motor skill performance within the limits of his experiment. Mental practice was most effective in combination with physical practice.

Twining (1949) found that both physical and mental practice produced significant improvement in the ring toss. Sheldon (1963) found no difference between the mental practice group and the physical group in improving the efficiency of the breast stroke in swimming. In studying the effects of three combinations of mental and physical practice Wilson (1961) found no between-group differences in learning the forehand and backhand drives in tennis. Maxwell (1968) found no difference between mental practice, physical practice, or a combination of mental and physical practice in learning the overhead volleyball serve.

Cotten and Nixon (1968) compared two methods of teaching the tennis serve. One group began serving at the service line and gradually moved back to the base line while the other group began serving from the base line in the traditional manner. The study showed no significant differences between the two teaching methods.

IMPLICATIONS FOR METHODS OF TEACHING

Bracewell (1968) used fifty-four kindergarten children to compare the demonstration method of teaching with the verbal instruction method. He found the difference in the ability of the experimental group to throw significantly better than the control group. Winslade (1963) found that both live demonstrations and 8-mm color film of basketball skills will improve skills in ninth-grade boys. Tuck (1965) found that the use of a laboratory demonstration with the use of animals was a high motivational factor in stimulating and keeping interest in the instruction of a health education unit on nutrition.

An early study by Ruffa (1936) tried to determine the effectiveness of motion pictures in teaching the high jump, broad jump, shot put, football throw, and the 100-yard dash. He concluded that the slow-motion film group learned more rapidly than the lecture-demonstration group.

Naylor (1963) found the part method superior to the whole method for tasks requiring complex perceptual skills and low interrelationships among task dimensions. In a further study, Pechstein (1918) found the part method of learning nonsensical syllables and mazes superior to the whole method and that the progressive-part method was consistently the most effective throughout the various learning tests. Stroud (1932) found the part and progressive-part methods significantly superior to the whole method in memorizing poetry.

In comparing the progressive-part method and the whole method of instruction in teaching basketball shooting skills to high school boys, House found that the progressive-part method was superior when instruction was given twice a week for ten weeks but that the whole method was superior when instruction was given twice a week for five weeks.

In a study comparing part-task vs. whole-task for teaching a problem-solving skill to first-graders, Anderson (1968) found that it was better to do a problem by parts than to attack the whole problem at once.

Prudy (1967) found that the whole-learning method was significantly superior to the part-whole method in the acquisition of accuracy and general golf ability. McGuigan (1955) found that the whole method of learning rifle marksmanship was superior to the part method. Shay (1934) found the whole method to be superior to the part method in learning the kip on the horizontal bar.

Wickstrom (1958) compared two methods of instruction, the whole method and the whole-direct repetitive method. He found that with one exception there were no significant differences in the results achieved using the two methods. The one exception was the back roll-snap down in favor of the whole method. Combs (1932) found that the whole-part-whole method was advantageous for teaching the hurdles, the whole method was slightly superior in teaching the shot put, and the whole-part-whole method was superior to the whole method in speed in learning complex motor activities.

Wyness (1963) compared the lecture-demonstration method with three variations of the use of motion picture films for improving shot put performance. He concluded that all groups improved in the skill of putting the shot, but none of the groups improved significantly more than the others.

Irwin (1958) studied the sound film-filmstrip method, the silent loop film method, and the verbal instruction method in the teaching of beginning tennis skills and knowledge. Her results showed that all three methods of teaching were equally effective in improving tennis playing ability and knowledge.

Douglas (1963) conducted a study to compare the effectiveness of loop movies and the explanation-demonstration methods of teaching wrestling. There was no significant difference between the two groups, however, a jury of experts who rated the wrestling performances commented that the explanation-demonstration group appeared to perform better than the loop movies group.

In an early study Pechstein (1917) investigated maze learning by humans and rats using the part and whole method. He found no significant differences between the two methods. Knapp (1952) found that when compared to the whole method, a combination of whole and part methods does not secure the more efficient learning in juggling. Goldsmith (1970) found no difference between the whole and the part-whole method in improving juggling or in the ability to retain the skill. Bro (1954) found no significant differences between the traditional and progressive-part methods of learning the side stroke.

In a study to compare the effectiveness of the lecture method and a small-group discussion method in teaching high school biology, Taylor (1959) found that high school biology students achieve the same amount of knowledge whether taught by the lecture method or group discussion method. In comparing the effectiveness of problem-solving, lecture, and discussion methods, Veekkler and Ismail (1962) concluded that the three approaches were equally effective.

Hamerslough (1972) concluded that reading, observing a film, or listening to a recording followed by mental rehearsal was ineffective in increasing performance in the complex motor skills of softball windmill pitch, golf chip shot, or soccer dribble.

IMPLICATIONS FOR TEACHING DESIGNS

In a study of different methods of instruction and practice on the acquisition of juggling, Wills (1970) compared oral instruction with demonstration, oral instruction and loop film instruction, written instruction, and written instruction and loop film instruction, each followed by physical or mental and physical practice. He found that oral instruction with demonstration followed by physical practice resulted in the greatest skill acquisition. Written instruction with loop film and oral instruction with loop film followed by physical practice ranked second and third respectively.

Shevlin (1968) tried to determine the effectiveness between the use of programmed materials and traditional classroom methods in the instruction of alcohol education for high school students. He found that programmed materials and techniques can be effectively used in the teaching of health education, as the experimental group learned significantly more than the control group.

Revines (1961) studied the effects of motor skill acquisition and retention of teaching by demonstration and practice, with and without accompanying verbal description and explanation. He found that verbal instructions had no significant effect on the amount of practice required to relearn the skill achieved prior to a non-practice interval, the amount of recall after an eight week non-practice interval, or the amount of practice required to learn a task. Verbal instruction in skill form did, however, tend to increase the knowledge of the form used.

Surburg (1968) in a study to investigate the effectiveness of mental practice in combination with three variables of instruction—audio, visual, and audio-visual—concluded that all three forms of instruction combined with mental practice improved execution of the motor skill. The best method appeared to be audio presentation and mental practice.

Petsch (1971) found that demonstration-practice improves kinesthetic learning statistically more than does reading-mental-practice, reading-practice, or reading-demonstration-practice. In comparing the individually prescribed instructional system with a traditional method in teaching badminton, Melville (1972) found that the individually prescribed instructional group was superior in the clear, serve, and drop shot, to the traditionally taught group.

Mariani (1970) compared the command and task method in teaching the forehand and backhand stroke in tennis. He found that the task method was superior in teaching the backhand but found no difference between the two teaching styles in the forehand stroke. However, in the retention of the two skills, the task method group showed a significantly greater retention for both strokes.

In a study to compare the traditional method of instruction with the movement exploration method of instruction in nonmajor skills classes, Croom (1972) found that the traditional method was more effective in improving general motor ability for college freshman women.

Pohl (1972) found that the combined use of the videotape method and the verbal coaching procedure was more favorable in teaching the high jump than was verbal instruction only, or videotape only.

Plese (1968) compared videotape replay instruction with a traditional approach in the teaching of gymnastic skills. He found that an immediate analysis of a motor performance by using videotape instant replay was significantly better than conventional instruction consisting of verbal explanation, demonstration, practice, instructor analysis, and correction.

Ward (1972) investigated the expository method and the guided discovery method in teaching college women beginning golf. She found that skill results favored the guided discovery group.

Berendsen (1967) conducted a study to determine the effects of teaching through movement description in combination with structural practice drills and with structural problem solving on learning basic tennis skills. He concluded that both methods are comparably effective in the acquisition of tennis skills but that the problem-solving method was more effective in the acquisition of knowledge about the game of tennis.

Doto (1972) investigated guided discovery and problem-solving situations to demonstrate the teaching of such concepts as the use of various golf clubs, offensive maneuvers in soccer, the components of vaulting, the physical attributes to be developed in weight training, and offensive strategy in basketball. He concluded that by structuring the discovery situation so that the student may experience success in his attempts to learn, the student will be motivated to attempt solutions to problems.

Garland (1960) studied the effectiveness of the problem-solving method in learning swimming. It was concluded that problem solving as a method of teaching swimming was effective and that it produced increased motivation and self-direction and produced greater comfort in water than did traditional methods.

In a study of the problem-solving method in teaching bowling, Laplante (1965) concluded that the problem-solving method of teaching bowling improves attitudes and interest, but does not significantly affect skill development.

Kaplan (1963) attempted to determine the effectiveness of television and problem solving in health education among college freshmen. He found that those having televised instruction showed significant gains in factual information, problem solving, and course grade while the problem-solving group tended to express more favorable attitudes toward the course than did the control group.

Russell (1967) found that the problem-solving method was more effective than the traditional method and that skilled performers could be negatively influenced by the traditional method in learning a motor skill.

Nicholson (1970) studied the relative effectiveness of televised instruction on body conditioning. Although subjects expressed a preference for personal rather than televised instruction, the results indicated that televised instruction was just as effective for body conditioning.

In comparing the creative teaching method and the traditional teaching method while teaching the 50-yard dash and the high jump, Hill (1970) found no difference between performance scores in the two methods. Engram (1970) found no difference between the traditional and the movement exploration method of teaching synchronized swimming. Schlott (1970) found no difference between the problem-solving method and the explanation-demonstration-execution method in field hockey.

IMPLICATIONS FOR
ORGANIZATIONS FOR LEARNING

Scott (1967) compared the formal and informal methods of teaching physical education to first-grade children. He found that the informal method was more effective in the development of creative ability than the formal method but that there was no difference between the two methods in perceptual motor development and physical fitness. Whilden (1956) found that a teacher-dominated group exhibited better command of the basic skills in beginning basketball while the pupil-dominated group performed better as a team.

Merki and others (1968) attempted to determine the value of a student-centered method for antismoking education as compared to a mass communication method (pamphlets and posters). They found that the student-centered group had a lower percentage rate than did the mass communication group at the end of the experimental period. Weesner (1972) found that the student-centered approach produced satisfaction in teaching fitness in college women while the teacher-directed classes participated to a greater extent in physical activity outside of class.

Irwin and others (1970) conducted a study to determine the relative effectiveness of the individual study approach, the peer-led approach, and the teacher-led approach in the instruction of a unit on smoking. They concluded that the individual approach was the most successful, showing the need to avoid the traditional authoritarian role of the teacher, which was the least successful approach.

Gustafson (1972), in a study of the effects of modular open-block scheduling on student attitudes, found that programmed instruction developed positive attitudes in physical education and increased motor fitness and motor ability. Thorpe and others (1971) found that in beginning badminton, students were superior taught by the traditional method of scheduling than by the master class plan where two or three classes met together with a master teacher once a week and in their regular class twice a week.

Holt and others (1970) compared the effectiveness of the Silvia Method and the Red Cross method of teaching beginning swimming. They found that group performances differed significantly in favor of the Silvia method on the distance tests and the survival time tests. In addition, the subjects who were taught by the Silvia method required fewer days to pass the Red Cross combined skills tests; however, there was not a significant difference in the percentage of subjects who learned how to swim.

Cross (1937) found that the whole method was superior in relatively simple tests, the minor game method was superior in tests which involved basketball skills that lent themselves to practice in lead-up game situations, and the whole-part method was superior in skills which demanded greater muscular coordination.

Young (1966) compared the readiness organization and traditional logical

organization in teaching field hockey to girls. She found that the readiness organization appeared to be more effective in terms of skill performance; however
there was no significant difference between the two organizations in knowledge
achievement.

Donaho (1972) compared the competition, readiness, and logical organizations in learning girls basketball. She found that the readiness and logical unit
organizations were more effective for teaching basketball skills to girls than the
competition unit organization while the readiness organization was more effective
for teaching basketball knowledge than the competition organization.

Grimland (1972) found that general motor ability increased following the
logical and competition organizations, while acquired tennis skill is least retained
twelve weeks after instruction using the competition organization. He found no
difference in retention of tennis knowledge using any of the three organizations
and that the three organizations had little effect on the general attitude of college
males toward physical activity. The logical organization resulted in less post-
participation in tennis and failed to produce an increase of confidence in tennis
skill after completion of the course.

Gordon (1963) investigated the effect of a programmed textbook on student learning and reactions regarding 16-mm motion picture projection principles and projector operation skills. When students used the programmed textbook with visual aids for learning of principles, they learned more in less time
and reacted more favorably to the method employed than did the lecture with
demonstration group. When students used the programmed textbook with visuals
they had difficulty transferring skills information from the book to the machine
and showed no advantage over the other group in actual learning of projector
operation or in use of training session time.

Neuman and Singer (1968) compared the traditional and programmed
learning methods on the acquisition of general tennis skills, playing ability, and
form. No difference was found between the groups in general skill, but the traditionally taught group improved significantly in general skills while the programmed group did not. The programmed group, however, received better subjective rating scores on form than did the traditionally taught group.

Farrell (1970) compared the effects of a programmed method for basic
instruction in the tennis forehand and backhand drives with the traditional
teacher-directed methods. No differences were found between the two groups;
however, it appeared that in beginning tennis classes different skill levels would
benefit from different instructional methods.

Appleton (1970) found no difference between the part method and the
cumulative method in learning modern dance composition. Davies (1971)
found no significant differences between the whole and part methods of teaching
handball to eleventh-grade boys. Cox (1970) found no difference between the
group taught by continuous concept sequencing and the group taught by discrete
concept sequencing. Also he concluded that the use of instant videotape had
no significant effect in stimulating students to learn the complex motor skills in
wrestling.

REFERENCES

ANDERSON, BRUCE D. "The Influence of Model Performances and Feedback on the Learning of a Complex Motor Skill." *Completed Research in Health, Physical Education, and Recreation* 12 (1970), 150.

ANDERSON, RICHARD. "Part-Task versus Whole-Task Procedures for Teaching a Problem-Solving Skill to First-Graders." *Journal of Educational Psychology* 59 (June, 1968), 210–14.

APPLETON, ELIZABETH A. "A Study of Experimentation in Two Different Methods of Teaching Modern Dance Composition." *Completed Research in Health, Physical Education, and Recreation* 12 (1970), 150.

BATTIG, WILLIAM F. "The Effect of Kinesthetic, Verbal, and Visual Cues on the Acquisition of a Lever-Positioning Skill." *Journal of Experimental Psychology* 50 (May, 1954), 371–79.

———. "Transfer from Verbal Pretraining to Motor Performance as a Function of Motor Task Complexity." *Journal of Experimental Psychology* 51 (June, 1956), 371–78.

BECKOW, PAUL A. *A Comparison of the Effectiveness of Mental Practice upon the Learning of Two Gross Motor Skills.* Microcarded. University of Oregon, 1944.

BERENDSEN, CAROL A. *The Relative Effectiveness of Descriptive Teaching and Structured Problem Solving in Learning Basic Tennis Skills.* Microcarded. University of Oregon, 1967.

BRACEWELL, MICHAEL B. "A Comparison of the Effectiveness of Two Methods of Teaching a Gross Motor Skill." Ph.D. diss., University of Oregon, 1968.

BRIGHTWELL, D. SHELBY. "Effect of Coeducational and Segregated Classes on Tennis Achievement." *Research Quarterly* 40 (May, 1969), 262–65.

BRO, L. V. "A Comparison of the Traditional and the Progressive-Part Methods of Learning the Side Stroke." Master's thesis, University of Iowa, 1954.

BROWN, H. STEVEN, and LLOYD MESSERSMITH. "An Experiment in Teaching Tumbling with and without Motion Pictures." *Research Quarterly* 19 (July, 1948), 304–7.

BROWN, PATRICIA D. "The Effect of Augmenting Instruction with an Improvised Teaching Aid for College Women in Learning Selected Badminton Skills." *Completed Research in Health, Physical Education, and Recreation* 12 (1970), 107.

BURNS, PATRICIA L. "The Effect of Physical Practice, Mental Practice, and Mental-Physical Practice on the Development of a Motor Skill." Master's thesis, Pennsylvania State University, 1962.

CAMP, BARBARA A. "The Effects of Viewing Loop Films on Tennis Skill and Form." Master's thesis, North Texas State University, May, 1969.

CARMICHAEL, GEORGE A. "Videotape Instant Replay as a Teaching Technique in Beginning Bowling Classes." *Completed Research in Health, Physical Education, and Recreation* 12 (1970), 264.

CHUI, EDWARD F. "A Study of Golf-o-Tron Utilization as a Teaching Aid in Relation to Improvement and Transfer." *Research Quarterly* 36 (May, 1965), 147–52.

CLARK, L. VERDELL. "The Effect of Mental Practice on the Development of a Certain Motor Skill." *Research Quarterly* 31 (December, 1960), 560–69.

COMBS, LEXY V. "A Comparison of the Efficiency of the Whole Method and of the Whole-Part Method of Teaching Track Activities." Master's thesis, University of Iowa, 1932.

COMREY, ANDREW L. "Group Performance in a Manual Dexterity Task." *The Journal of Applied Psychology* 37 (June, 1953), 207–10.

CONRY, BARBARA JANE. "Effectiveness of the Use of Video Tapes in Learning Beginning Fencing." Master's thesis, University of Washington, 1969.

CORBIN, CHARLES B. "Effects of Covert Rehearsal on the Development of a Complex Motor Skill." *Journal of General Psychology* 76 (March, 1967), 143–50.

———. "Effects of Mental Practice on Skill Development after Controlled Practice." *Research Quarterly* 38 (December, 1967), 534–38.

COTTEN, DOYICE J., and JANE NIXON. "A Comparison of Two Methods of Teaching the Tennis Serve." *Research Quarterly* 39 (December, 1968), 929–32.

COX, KENNETH. "An Experiment in Teaching Complex Motor Skills to University Freshman Male Students Using Continuous and Discrete Concept Sequences with and without Instant Videotape Replay." *Completed Research in Health, Physical Education, and Recreation* 12 (1970), 255.

CROOM, ANNIE P. "A Comparison of the Effects of Two Methods of Teaching Movement Fundamentals upon General Motor Ability." *Completed Research in Health, Physical Education, and Recreation* 14 (1972), 115.

CROSS, THOMAS J. "A Comparison of the Whole Method, the Minor-Game Method, and the Whole-Part Method of Teaching Basketball to Ninth-Grade Boys." *Research Quarterly* 8 (December, 1937), 49–54.

DANIEL, WILLIAM, and PETER MURDOCH. "Effectiveness of Learning from a Programmed Text Compared with a Conventional Text Covering the Same Material." *Journal of Educational Psychology* 59 (December, 1968), 425–31.

DAVIES, DONALD B. "A Comparative Study of the Whole and Part Methods of Teaching Handball to Beginning Students. Microcarded. Ph.D. diss., University of Oregon, 1971.

DAVIES, DOROTHY R. "The Effect of Tuition upon the Process of Learning a Complex Motor Skill." *Journal of Educational Psychology* 36 (September, 1945), 352–65.

DEESE, JAMES, and ROGER A. KAUFMAN. "Serial Effects in Recall of Unorganized and Sequentially Organized Verbal Material." *Journal of Experimental Psychology* 54 (September, 1957), 180–87.

DEL RAY, PATRICIA M. "The Effect of Videotaped Feedback and Environmental Certainty on Form, Accuracy, and Latency during Skill Acquisition." Ph.D. diss., Queens College, 1970.

DONAHO, PATSY M. "A Comparison of the Effectiveness of Three Unit Organizational Schemes in Teaching Girls' Basketball." Master's thesis, Texas A&M University, 1972.

DOTO, FRANK. "An Analysis of the Discovery Process in Teaching Concepts Related to Physical Activities Based on an Interpretation of Festinger's Theory of Cognitive Dissonance." *Completed Research in Health, Physical Education, and Recreation* 14 (1972), 148.

DOUGLAS, JOHN G., JR. "The Value and Limitations of Loop Movies in the Teaching of Wrestling Maneuvers." Master's thesis, University of Massachusetts, 1963.

DOWELL, LINUS J. "Game Strategy Apprehension of Athletes and Non-Athletes in a Competitive and Cooperative Learning Environment." A Paper presented at the Research Section of the American Association of Health, Physical Education, and Recreation National Convention, Minneapolis, 1973.

DRESSER, CLYDA JANE. "The Value of a Loop Film in Teaching the Crawl Stroke." Master's thesis, University of Colorado, May, 1961.

DROWATZKY, JOHN N. "Television Augmented Feedback in Learning a Balance Skill." Ph.D. diss., University of Toledo, 1971.

DUNHAM, PAUL LOUIS, JR. "The Effect of Serial versus Sequence Practice on Performance Level. PhD. diss., University of Arkansas, 1968.

EGSTROM, GLEN H. "Effects of an Emphasis on Conceptualizing Techniques during Early Learning of a Gross Motor Skill." *Research Quarterly* 38 (December, 1964), 562–69.

ENGRAM, CAROL. "A Comparison of Two Methods of Teaching Synchronized Swimming." *Completed Research in Health, Physical Education, and Recreation* 12 (1970), 220–21.

FARRELL, JOAN E. "Programmed versus Teacher-Directed Instruction in Beginning Tennis for Women." *Research Quarterly* 41 (March, 1970), 51–56.

FOWLER, JOYCE. "The Value of the Slow-Motion Film as an Instructional Aid in the Teaching of Tennis Skills." Master's thesis, University of North Carolina, May, 1955.

GANSEL, ALICE K. "The Effect of Limited Visibility in Teaching Women Bowlers Spot Bowling." *Completed Research in Health, Physical Education, and Recreation* 13 (1971), 118.

GARLAND, IRIS. "Effectiveness of Problem-Solving Method in Learning Swimming." Master's thesis, University of California, 1960.

GODLASKY, CHARLES A. "An Experimental Study to Determine the Relative Effectiveness of Two Methods of Teaching the Crawl Stroke in Swimming." Master's thesis, The Pennsylvania State University, 1955.

GOLDSMITH, BARRY. "A Comparison of Whole and Part-Whole Methods of Improving Juggling and the Ability to Retain the Skill." *Completed Research in Health, Physical Education, and Recreation* 12 (1970), 80.

GORDON, ROGER L. "An Investigation of the Effect of a Programmed Instructional Method on Skill Learning in Audiovisual Education." Ph.D. diss., Michigan State University, 1963.

GRAY, CHARLES A., and WAYNE B. BRUMBACH. "Effect of Daylight Projection of Film Loops on Learning Badminton." *Research Quarterly* 38 (December, 1967), 562–69.

GREBNER, FLORENCE D. "Effectiveness of Two Methods of Attaining a Full Draw by Beginning Archers." *Research Quarterly* 40 (March, 1969), 50–54.

GREEN, JOHN M. "The Effect of Television Replay as a Technique in Teaching Beginning Swimming Skills." *Completed Research in Health, Physical Education, and Recreation* 13 (1971), 76.

GRIMLAND, ANDREW C. "The Effects of Selected Teaching Styles on Learning an Individual Sport." Ph.D. diss., Texas A&M University, 1972.

GUSTAFSON, JOHN. "The Effects of Programmed Instruction and Modular Open-block Scheduling on Student Attitude toward Physical Education." Ph.D. diss., University of Utah, 1972.

HALVERSON, TOLAS E. "A Comparison of Three Methods of Teaching Motor Skills." Master's thesis, University of Wisconsin, January, 1949.

HAMERSLOUGH, WALTER S. "The Effectiveness of Three Methods of Instruction, Followed by Mental Rehearsal, in Learning Three Complex Gross Motor Tasks." *Completed Research in Health, Physical Education and Recreation* 14 (1972), 180.

HAMMER, GEORGE J., and GLORIA M. NATALE. "Initial Learning of a Motor Skill without Involvement." *Journal of Business Education* 39 (April, 1964), 282–83.

HARLESS, IVAN L. "A Comparison of Improvement of Selected Motor Skills Utilizing Two Instructional Methods." *Completed Research in Health, Physical Education, and Recreation* 12 (1970), 133.

HAWTHORNE, MARTHA ELLEN. "A Study of the Effectiveness of the Slow-Motion Picture in Teaching Golf." Master's thesis, Louisiana State University, May, 1961.

HENSCHEN, KEITH P. "The Effects of a Small Basket upon Basketball Shooting Accuracy with the Nondominant Hand." *Completed Research in Health, Physical Education, and Recreation* 14 (1972), 108.

HILL, SANDRA L. "A Comparative Investigation of Creative and Traditional Teaching Methods in Track and Field." *Completed Research in Health, Physical Education, and Recreation* 12 (1970), 87.

HIXSON, CHALMER G. "Utilization of Portable Video Tape Recorder in Physical Education." *The Physical Education Newsletter* 15 (October, 1970), 5.

HOLT, ALYCE, JOANNE THORPE, and LAURENCE HOLT. "Two Methods of Teaching Beginning Swimming." *Research Quarterly* 41 (October, 1970), 371–77.

HORNAK, JAMES E. "The Effects of Three Methods of Teaching on the Learning of a Motor Skill." *Completed Research in Health, Physical Education, and Recreation* 14 (1972), 172.

HOUSE, GERALD WILLIAM. "A Comparison of the Progressive-Part Method and the Whole Method in Teaching Basketball Shooting Skills to High School Boys." Master's thesis, University of Alabama, 1944.

HUFFMAN, EMOGENE. "A Study of the Effects of Mental Practice on Motor Learning." Master's thesis, University of Colorado, January, 1954.

HUFFTY, ANDREW E. "Relative Effectiveness of Teaching A Gymnastic Skill Using the Instant Replay Video Tape Recorder." *Abstract of Research Papers*, 1970 AAHPER Convention, Seattle, 1970, p. 108.

IRWIN, JUNE. "The Effect of Selected Audio-Visual Aids on Teaching Beginning

Tennis Skills and Knowledge to College Women." Ph.D. diss., Indiana University, May, 1958.

IRWIN, R. P., W. H. CRESWELL, and D. J. STAUFFER. "The Effect of the Teacher and Three Different Classroom Approaches on Seventh-Grade Students' Knowledge, Attitudes and Beliefs about Smoking." *Journal of School Health* 40 (September, 1970), 355–59.

JARVIS, LINDLE. "Effects of Self-Instructive Materials in Learning Selected Motor Skills." *Research Quarterly* 38 (December, 1967), 623–29.

JOHNSTON, WILLIAM A. "Transfer of Team Skills as a Function of Type of Training." *Journal of Applied Psychology* 50 (April, 1966), 102–8.

JONES, JOHN G. "Motor Learning Without Demonstration of Physical Practice, under Two Conditions of Mental Practice." *Research Quarterly* 36 (October, 1965), 270–76.

KAPLAN, ROBERT. "Effectiveness of Television and Problem Solving in Health Education." *Journal of School Health* 33 (April, 1963), 179–85.

KARLIN, LAWRENCE, and RUDOLF G. MORTIMER. "Effects of Visual and Verbal Cues on Learning a Motor Skill." *Journal of Experimental Psychology* 64 (December, 1962), 608–14.

KAYE, RICHARD A. "The Use of Waist-Type Flotation Device as an Adjunct in Teaching Beginning Swimming Skills." *Research Quarterly* 36 (October, 1965), 277–81.

KELSEY, IAN B. "Effects of Mental and Physical Practice on Muscular Endurance." *Research Quarterly* 32 (March, 1961), 47–53.

KINGSLEY, JOAN L. "The Effectiveness of Teaching Large Motor Skills by the Spaced-Unit Method as Compared with the Continuous-Unit Method." *Completed Research in Health, Physical Education, and Recreation* 13 (1971), 139.

KNAPP, CLYDE G., and W. ROBERT DIXON. "Learning to Juggle: II. A Study of Whole and Part Methods." *Research Quarterly* 23 (December, 1952), 398–401.

LAPLANTE, MARILYN. "A Study of the Problem-Solving Method of Teaching Bowling." Master's thesis, University of North Carolina, 1965.

LAYTON, TERRY W. "The Effect of a Basketball Training Glove on Shooting Accuracy." *Completed Research in Health, Physical Education, and Recreation* 14 (1972), 133.

LINDEBURG, FRANKLIN A., and JACK E. HEWITT. "Effect of an Oversized Basketball on Shooting Ability and Ball Handling." *Research Quarterly* 36 (May, 1965), 164–67.

LOCKHART, AILEENE. "The Value of the Motion Picture as an Instructional Device in Learning a Motor Skill." *Research Quarterly* 15 (May, 1944), 181–87.

LONDEREE, BEN R., JR. "Effect of Training with Motion Pictures versus Flash Cards upon Football Play Recognition." *Research Quarterly* 38 (May, 1967), 202–7.

LUNDQUIST, ALEXANDER T. "Immediate Knowledge of Results via Videotape Replay and Its Effect on the Learning of Selected Football Skills." *Completed Research in Health, Physical Education, and Recreation* 11 (1969), 195.

MACFARLANE, DORIS J. "A Comparison of Two Methods of Teaching the Forehand Tennis Stroke to Nine- and Ten-Year-Olds." *Completed Research in Health, Physical Education, and Recreation* 13 (1971), 336.

MALINA, ROBERT M. "Effects of Varied Information Feedback Practice Conditions on Throwing Speed and Accuracy." *Research Quarterly* 40 (March, 1969), 134–45.

MARIANI, TOM. "A Comparison of the Effectiveness of the Command Method and the Task Method." *Research Quarterly* 41 (May, 1970), 171–74.

MATTHEWS, DONALD K., and JOE MCDANIEL. "Effectiveness of Using Golf-Lite in Learning Golf Swing." *Research Quarterly* 33 (October, 1962), 488–91.

MAXWELL, JOAN M. "The Effect of Mental Practice on the Learning of the Overhead Volleyball Serve." Master's thesis, Central Missouri State College, July, 1968.

MCCATTY, CRESSY A. M. "Effects of the Use of a Flotation Device in Teaching Nonswimmers." *Research Quarterly* 39 (1966), 621–26.

MCGUIGAN, F. J., and EUGENE F. MACCASLIN. "Whole and Part Methods in Learning a Perceptual Motor Skill." *American Journal of Psychology* 68 (December, 1955), 658–61.

MEGALE, DONALD M. "Rhythmic Accompaniment as a Teaching Aid in the Development of Elementary Sport Skills." *Abstracts of Research Papers,* 1972 AAHPER Convention, Houston, 1972, 115.

MELVILLE, DONALD S. "A Comparison of the Acquisition of Badminton Skills of College Students between the Individually Prescribed Instructional System and a Traditional Method." *Completed Research in Health, Physical Education, and Recreation* 14 (1972), 207.

MERKI, D. J., et al. "The Effects of Two Educational Methods and Message Themes on Rural Youth Smoking Behavior." *Journal of School Health* 38 (October, 1968), 448–54.

MEYER, DAVID C. "Videotape and Skill Learning." *Educational Technology* 9 (November, 1969), 79–82.

MINAERT, WALTER A. "An Analysis of the Value of Dry-Skiing in Learning Selected Skiing Skills." *Research Quarterly* 21 (March, 1950), 42–52.

MITCHELL, FRANCES P. "A Study of the Relative Effectiveness of Mental Practice, Physical Practice, and a Combination of Mental and Physical Practice in Learning the Long Serve Used in Badminton." Master's thesis, University of Colorado, May, 1956.

MOHR, DOROTHY R., and MILDRED E. BARRETT. "Effect of Knowledge of Mechanical Principles in Learning to Perform Intermediate Swimming Skills." *Research Quarterly* 33 (December, 1962), 574–80.

MOORE, BALLARD J. "Evaluation of a Pictorial Form of Instructional Aid in the Teaching of a Motor Skill." *Completed Research in Health, Physical Education, and Recreation* 13 (1971), 129.

MORGAN, NANCY A. "Comparison of Verbal and Visual Cues in Teaching Beginning Swimming." *Research Quarterly* 42 (December, 1971), 431–35.

NAYLOR, JAMES C., and GEORGE E. BRIGGS. "Effects of Task Complexity and Task Organization in the Relative Efficiency of Part and Whole Training Methods." *Journal of Experimental Psychology* 65 (March, 1963), 217–24.

NELSON, DALE O. "Effects of Slow-Motion Loop Films on the Learning of Golf." *Research Quarterly* 29 (March, 1958), 37–45.

NELSON, RICHARD C., JANET DAILEY, and JANET A. WESSEL. "Effectiveness of a Bowling Aid to University Bowling Instruction." *Research Quarterly* 34 (May, 1963), 136–43.

NEUMAN, MILTON C., and ROBERT N. SINGER. "A Comparison of Traditional versus Programmed Methods of Learning Tennis." *Research Quarterly* 39 (December, 1968), 1044–48.

NICHOLS, BEVERLY A. "A Comparison of Two Methods of Developing the Overhand

Throw for Distance in Four-, Five-, Six-, and Seven-Year-Old Children." *Completed Research in Health, Physical Education, and Recreation* 14 (1972), 116.

NICHOLSON, MARTHA K. "The Relative Effectiveness of Personal and Televised Instruction in Body Conditioning." Ph.D. diss., University of Washington, 1970.

NYCE, LAWRENCE G. "The Effects of a Lightweight Bowling Ball upon Various Stages of Learning of Beginning Bowlers." *Completed Research in Health, Physical Education, and Recreation* 14 (1972), 145.

PECHSTEIN, L. A. "Alleged Elements of Waste in Learning a Motor Problem by the Part Method." *Journal of Educational Psychology* 7 (May, 1917), 303–10.

———. "Whole versus Part Methods in Learning Nonsensical Syllables." *Journal of Educational Psychology* 9 (June, 1918), 381–87.

PENMAN, DOUGLAS A., DOUGLAS BAURTZ, and REX DAVIS. "Relative Effectiveness of an Instant Replay Videotape Recorder in Teaching Trampoline." *Research Quarterly* 39 (December, 1968), 1062–67.

PENMAN, KENNETH. "Relative Effectiveness of Teaching Beginning Tumbling with and without an Instant Videotape Recorder." *Perceptual and Motor Skills* (February, 1969), 45–46.

PETSCH, VERL E. "Comparison of Selected Instructional Techniques Involved in Learning a Simple Skill of Kinesthetic Balance." *Completed Research in Health, Physical Education, and Recreation* 13 (1971), 90.

PLESE, ELLIOT RAY. "A Comparison of Videotape Replay with a Traditional Approach in the Teaching of Selected Gymnastic Skills." *Completed Research in Health, Physical Education, and Recreation* 10 (1968), 74–75.

POHL, PATRICK L. "Relative Effectiveness of Using Videotape Feedback in Teaching the High Jump." *Completed Research in Health, Physical Education and Recreation* 14 (1972) 127.

PRIEBE, ROY E., and WILLIAM H. BURTON. "The Slow-Motion Picture as a Coaching Device." *The School Review* 47 (March, 1939), 192–98.

PRUDY, BONNIE J., and MARY L. STALLARD. "Effect of Two Learning Methods and Two Grips on the Acquisition of Power and Accuracy in the Golf Swing of College Women." *Research Quarterly* 38 (October, 1967), 480–84.

REID, DIANNE. "The Effect of the Use of the Videotape Recorder as an Aid in Teaching the Volleyball Serve." *Completed Research in Health, Physical Education, and Recreation* 13 (1971), 168.

REILLY, JEAN A. "A Comparison of Instructional Emphasis of Speed, Accuracy, and Speed and Accuracy upon the Performance of the Beginning Fencer." *Completed Research in Health, Physical Education, and Recreation* 13 (1971), 135.

REVINES, RICHARD S. "Effects on Motor Skill Acquisition and Retention of Teaching by Demonstration with and without Verbal Explanation." Master's thesis, Pennsylvania State University, 1961.

RHEA, HAROLD C. "The Value of Video Self-Analysis as a Reinforcement Technique for Learning When Substituted for Actual Practice of Gross Motor Skills." Ph.D. diss., Wake Forest University, 1970.

RUFFA, EDWARD J. "An Experimental Study of Motion Pictures as Used in the Teaching of Certain Athletic Skills." Master's thesis, Leland Stanford University, 1936.

RUSHALL, BRENT S., and JOHN PETTINGER. "An Evaluation of the Effect of Various Reinforcers Used as Motivators in Swimming." *Research Quarterly* 40 (October, 1969), 540–45.

RUSSELL, MARILYN. "Effectiveness of Problem-Solving Methods in Learning a Gross Motor Skill." Master's thesis, University of Washington, 1967.

SCHLOTT, KAREN O. "A Comparison of Two Methods of Teaching Selected Skills in Field Hockey." *Completed Research in Health, Physical Education, and Recreation* 12 (1970), 226.

SCOTT, ROBERT S. "A Comparison of Teaching Two Methods of Physical Education with Grade One Pupils." *Research Quarterly* 38 (March, 1967), 151–54.

SHAY, CLAYTON T. "The Progressive-Part *vs.* the Whole Method of Learning Motor Skills." *Research Quarterly* 5 (December, 1934), 62–67.

SHELDON, MIRIAM F. "An Investigation of the Relative Effects of Mental Practice and Physical Practice in Improving Efficiency of the Breast Stroke." Master's thesis. University of Oregon, 1963.

SHEVLIN, JULIUS. "Effectiveness of Programmed Materials in Teaching a Secondary School Health Education Unit." *Research Quarterly* 39 (October, 1968), 704–7.

SHICK, JACQUELINE. "Effects of Mental Practice on Selected Volleyball Skills for College Women." *Research Quarterly* 41 (March, 1970), 88–94.

SOLLEY, WILLIAM H., and SUSAN BORDERS. "Relative Effects of Two Methods of Teaching the Forehand Drive in Tennis." *Research Quarterly* 36 (March, 1965), 120–22.

SPENCER, PATRICIA. "Movies, Slides, and Demonstrations as Visual Aids for Teaching Movement Patterns. Master's thesis. University of Colorado, January, 1961.

STEBBINS, RICHARD J. "A Comparison of the Effects of Physical and Mental Practice in Learning a Motor Skill." *Research Quarterly* 39 (October, 1968), 714–20.

STROUD, J. B., and C. W. RIDGEWAY. "The Relative Efficiency of the Whole, Part, and Progressive-Part Methods When Trials Are Massed—A Minor Experiment." *Journal of Educational Psychology* 23 (November, 1932), 632–34.

SURBERG, PAUL R. "Audio, Visual, and Audio-Visual Instruction with Mental Practice in Developing the Forehand Tennis Drive." *Research Quarterly* 39 (October, 1968), 728–34.

TAKACS, ROBERT. "A Comparison of the Effect of Two Methods of Practice on Basketball Free-Throw Shooting." *Completed Research in Health, Physical Education, and Recreation* 8 (1966), 37.

TAYLOR, HAROLD. "A Comparison of the Effectiveness of a Lecture Method and a Small-Group Discussion Method of Teaching High School Biology." *Science Education* 43 (December, 1959), 442–46.

THOMPSON, DENNIS. "Immediate External Feedback in the Learning of Golf Skills." *Research Quarterly* 40 (October, 1969), 589–94.

THORPE, JOANNE, CHARLOTTE WEST, and DOROTHY DAVIES. "Learning under a Traditional and an Experimental Schedule Involving Master Classes." *Research Quarterly* 42 (February, 1971), 83–89.

TUCK, MIRIAM. "Experimental Demonstration as a Method of Stimulating Learning." *Journal of School Health* 35 (April, 1965), 172–85.

TUFTS, SHARON. "The Effects of Mental Practice on the Scores of Intermediate Bowlers." Master's thesis, Woman's College, University of North Carolina, 1963.

TWINING, WILBUR E. "Mental Practice and Physical Practice in Learning Motor Skill." *Research Quarterly* 20 (December, 1949), 432–34.

VEENKER, C. H., and A. H. ISMAIL. "Effectiveness of Three Approaches to College Health Instruction." *Research Quarterly* 33 (March, 1962), 129–35.

WARD, DIANNE S. "A Comparison of Two Teaching Methods in Beginning Golf: Expository versus Guided Discovery." *Completed Research in Health, Physical Education, and Recreation* 14 (1972), 170.

WATERLAND, JOAN C. *The Effects of Mental Practice Combined with Kinesthetic Perception When the Practice Precedes Each Overt Performance of a Motor Skill.* Master's thesis, University of Wisconsin, January, 1956.

WATKINS, DAVID L. "Motion Pictures as an Aid in Correcting Baseball Batting Faults." *Research Quarterly* 34 (May, 1963), 228–33.

WEBB, FLORENCE. "An Explanatory Study to Determine the Effects of the Number of Implicit Rehearsals and the Spacing of Rehearsals on the Learning of a Motor Skill." Ph.D. diss., University of Oregon, May, 1961.

WEEKS, AUDREY S. "Conceptualization in the Acquisition of Skill in Golf." *Completed Research in Health, Physical Education, and Recreation* 12 (1970), 217.

WEESNER, MARJORIE L. "A Comparison of Two Approaches in the Teaching of Conditioning and Their Effect upon the Fitness, Knowledge, and Attitude of College Women." *Completed Research in Health, Physical Education, and Recreation* 14 (1972), 186.

WHILDEN, PEGGY P. "Comparison of Two Methods of Teaching Beginning Basketball." *Research Quarterly* 27 (May, 1956), 235–42.

WICKSTROM, RALPH L. "Comparative Study of Methodologies for Teaching Gymnastics and Tumbling Stunts." *Research Quarterly* 29 (March, 1958), 109–15.

WILLS, KEITH C. "Effect of Different Methods of Instruction and Practice on Skill Acquisition of a Motor Task." Ph.D. diss., Texas A&M University, January, 1970.

———. "The Effect of Mental Practice and Physical Practice on Learning a Motor Skill." Master's thesis, Arkansas State University, May, 1965.

WILSON, MARGARET E. "The Relative Effect of Mental Practice and Physical Practice in Learning the Tennis Forehand and Backhand Drives." *Dissertation Abstracts* 21 (February, 1961), 1837.

WINSLADE, DONALD D. "The Effect of the 8-mm Slow-Motion Color Film on the Learning of Specific Motor Skills." Master's thesis, University of British Columbia, May, 1963.

WOODS, JOHN B. "The Effect of Varied Instructions Emphasis upon the Development of a Motor Skill." *Research Quarterly* 38 (March, 1967), 132–42.

WYATT, VIRGINIA. "The Effectiveness of Visual Cues and Kinesthetic Cues in the Teaching of the Overhand Throw to Seventh-Grade Girls." Master's thesis, University of Washington, 1969.

WYNESS, GERALD B. "A Study of the Effectiveness of Motion Picture Films as an Aid in Teaching a Gross Motor Skill." Ph.D. diss., University of Oregon, May, 1963.

YOUNG, EARLAINE. "A Comparison of Two Methods of Teaching Field Hockey to College Women." *Completed Research in Health, Physical Education, and Recreation* 8 (1966), 37.

INDEX